Letts

KS2 Success

Age 7-11

Grammar
Punctuation & Spelling

SATs
Practice Workbook

Practice Workbook

Shelley Welsh

Contents

Grammar Terms

Creating Sentences

Sentence Features

Punctuation

Vocabulary and Spelling

Mixed Practice Questions

Glossary

Answers
Set in a pull-out booklet in the centre of the book

Nouns

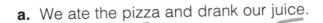

1 Underline the common **nouns** in these sentences.

a. We ate the pizza and drank our juice. **(1 mark)**

b. She swapped her book at the library. **(1 mark)**

c. He dropped lots of pencils on the floor. **(1 mark)**

d. The girls stopped talking and listened to their teacher. **(1 mark)**

e. Our school closed early because of the heavy snow. **(1 mark)**

f. Scarves, gloves and hats – all were packed for the trip. **(1 mark)**

Noun types

1 Explain why some of the words in this sentence start with a capital letter. **(1 mark)**

Last August, when Emilie went on holiday to Spain, she read *The Chronicles of Narnia*.

They are all proper nouns + at the start of the sentence

2 Underline **all** the common and proper nouns in the following sentences.

a. The ducks wandered down the road and into the field. **(1 mark)**

b. Our team finished early on Wednesday because of the snow. **(1 mark)**

c. Phil showed great courage when faced with the tiger. **(1 mark)**

d. Prince William visited Wales at the beginning of July. **(1 mark)**

e. My football hit the top bar of the net. **(1 mark)**

f. We went in the sea, although the weather was grim and the waves rough. **(1 mark)**

Expanded noun phrases

1 Underline all the **expanded noun phrases** in the following sentences.

a. The beautiful blue butterfly landed on my bare shoulder. **(1 mark)**

b. We showed a lot of courage in spite of the awful danger we were in. **(1 mark)**

c. My old grandfather kept two herds of cows on his five-acre farm. **(1 mark)**

d. Our local primary school has a well-stocked library full of interesting books. **(1 mark)**

e. Sasha went to the beautiful islands of Guernsey and Jersey for his first-ever holiday. **(1 mark)**

f. After eating cheese and ham sandwiches, my little sister and I headed home. **(1 mark)**

2 Add suitable determiners and adjectives to these nouns to create expanded noun phrases.
An example has been done for you. **(5 marks)**

puppy	The mischievous little puppy.
countryside	The bright green countryside.
determination	I played football with a lot of detmination.
disgust	I looked out the window in digust to see that it was raining.
ocean	✓ The deep blue ocean.
swarm	He was being chased by a big swarm

Remind your child that names of planets, mountains, rivers, countries, book titles, months of the year and days of the week are all proper nouns and therefore start with a capital letter.

Parent tip!

Total ___ 24

Identifying verbs

1 Underline the **verbs** in these sentences.
There may be more than one in each.

a. The fire roared in the dark night sky. **(1 mark)**

b. We left our towels on the beach. **(1 mark)**

c. The soldiers fire at the practice target. **(1 mark)**

d. The aim of the game is to aim high. **(1 mark)**

e. Somehow we always manage to forget someone! **(1 mark)**

f. When you have finished, start the next task. **(1 mark)**

Past and present tense

1 Put the verb on the left into the **present** and **past tenses**.
An example has been done for you. **(5 marks)**

Verb	Present	Past
to decide	*I am deciding/I decide*	*I decided/I was deciding*
to eat		
to be		
to know		
to go		
to admit		

2 Circle the **two** verbs in each of these sentences, then say
whether they are present or past tense.

a. We regularly go to the cinema on Fridays but last week
we were on holiday. **(1 mark)**

....

b. Our dog barks at strangers but you are well-known to him. **(1 mark)**

....

c. I often see your brother at football training but he wasn't there yesterday. **(1 mark)**

....

3 Change the verbs in these sentences into another form of the past tense.
An example has been done for you.

Mum rang the doctor for an appointment.

Mum was ringing the doctor for an appointment.

a. We enjoyed the performance tremendously.

Past: .... **(1 mark)**

b. The bright sun shone high in the clear blue sky.

Past: .... **(1 mark)**

Future tense

1 Rewrite these sentences by changing the verb in brackets into the **future tense**.

a. Tomorrow we (to swim) unless it rains. **(1 mark)**

....

b. In the summer, I (to sail) to Ireland. **(1 mark)**

....

c. After the tests, the children (to celebrate) with a party. **(1 mark)**

....

d. With the weather looking uncertain, we (to wear) our raincoats. **(1 mark)**

....

Total $\frac{}{20}$

Modals indicating possibility

1 Circle **two modal verbs** indicating **possibility** in each of these sentences.

    a. We may be going away tomorrow but Dad may not be able to come. **(1 mark)**

    b. Jon may play football this Saturday and if he does, he could be made team captain. **(1 mark)**

    c. There can be as many as fifty children in the pool at any given time; there could even be more. **(1 mark)**

    d. Joseph thought there might be heavy traffic so he asked if he could walk to school. **(1 mark)**

2 Insert appropriate modal verbs in these sentences.

    a. I .... go to the shops later; I haven't made my mind up yet. **(1 mark)**

    b. If the weather stays uncertain, we .... need to bring our waterproofs. **(1 mark)**

    c. It .... not be possible to change our plans about going to the cinema. **(1 mark)**

    d. It .... snow later according to the weather forecast. **(1 mark)**

3 Tick the question below that uses a modal verb to indicate there is a **possibility** that something will happen. **(1 mark)**

    a. Must you always copy my work? ☐

    b. Might you be coming to our house later? ☐

    c. You could have tried harder, couldn't you? ☐

    d. Would you let me know if you are walking to school? ☐

Adverbs to indicate possibility

1 Underline the **adverbs** in these sentences that range from **certainty** to **uncertainty**.

   a. We clearly aren't going to get there on time with this heavy traffic.   **(1 mark)**

   b. It's obviously the rush hour since it's 5 o'clock.   **(1 mark)**

   c. I certainly won't be coming at this time again.   **(1 mark)**

   d. Maybe we should have taken the country roads.   **(1 mark)**

2 Insert an appropriate adverb in each sentence to indicate certainty.

   a. You .... have to eat more healthily.   **(1 mark)**

   b. Sarim .... isn't going to come now.   **(1 mark)**

   c. .... the shop is closed at this time of night.   **(1 mark)**

   d. Erin .... has more homework to finish.   **(1 mark)**

3 Tick the correct box to indicate which adverbs in the paragraph below indicate **uncertainty** or **certainty**.   **(5 marks)**

> It's **unlikely** we will be moving house before the summer. The builders might have difficulties finding the bricks we want and will **possibly** have to import them from abroad. It's **definitely** been a difficult time for Mum and Dad who **clearly** wanted us to be in well before the start of the school year. They've not had a minute to themselves and **perhaps** they will think twice about such a big project in the future.

Adverb	Certainty	Uncertainty
unlikely		
possibly		
definitely		
clearly		
perhaps		

Total ——
22

Adjectives

1 Underline **two adjectives** in each sentence.

a. Freddy, that naughty boy in Year 2, was in
big trouble yet again. **(1 mark)**

b. With his new football in his hands, Archie headed
towards the muddy field. **(1 mark)**

c. Although Brogan was nervous about the test, he was
nonetheless a determined boy. **(1 mark)**

d. Despite the atrocious weather conditions, the well-known
team of explorers set off. **(1 mark)**

2 Rewrite these sentences to make them more interesting by
adding **one adjective** to describe **each noun**.

a. The cat slept on the mat. **(1 mark)**

....

....

b. My sister came in and sat on the armchair. **(1 mark)**

....

....

c. My mum cooked our dinner. **(1 mark)**

....

....

d. We came across a field full of flowers. **(1 mark)**

....

....

Adjectives comparing two nouns

① Turn the words in brackets into **adjectives that show a comparison** between the two nouns in each sentence.

a. Matt is (old) than Thomas.   **(1 mark)**

....

b. Freya's hair is (curly) than her big sister's.   **(1 mark)**

....

c. I think the countryside is (beautiful) than inner-city areas.   **(1 mark)**

....

d. Our homework was (interesting) this week than last week.   **(1 mark)**

....

Adjectives comparing more than two nouns

① Turn the words in brackets into suitable **adjectives that compare the subjects** in each sentence with everyone or everything else.

a. Mia had the (long) hair of all the girls in her class.   **(1 mark)**

....

b. That actress had to be the (fascinating) person I'd ever interviewed.   **(1 mark)**

....

c. We had the (intelligent) people on our quiz team.   **(1 mark)**

....

d. It was the (disgusting) meal we'd ever eaten.   **(1 mark)**

....

Total ____
16

Conjunctions that join two clauses of equal importance

1 Underline the **conjunctions** in the following sentences.

a. My mother likes to go to Spain on holiday but my father prefers France. **(1 mark)**

b. We couldn't make swimming tonight for our car wouldn't start. **(1 mark)**

c. I find long division really easy yet long multiplication really hard! **(1 mark)**

d. It was way past our bedtime so our parents sent us to bed. **(1 mark)**

e. We grabbed our swimsuits and set off for the swimming pool. **(1 mark)**

f. Kathy hadn't a clue where the map was, nor did she really care. **(1 mark)**

2 Link the following sentences together with an appropriate conjunction. You might need to replace nouns with pronouns.

a. Milo has a dog. Milo hasn't got a cat. **(1 mark)**

....

b. Seb likes carrots. Seb likes cabbage. **(1 mark)**

....

c. My sister is extremely tall. I am exceptionally short. **(1 mark)**

....

d. Millie is amazing at tennis. She struggles with badminton. **(1 mark)**

....

e. The rain was very heavy. The children couldn't play football. **(1 mark)**

....

Conjunctions that join a main clause to a subordinate clause

1 Circle or underline the **conjunctions** that join a main clause to a **subordinate clause** in the following sentences.

   a. Although it was snowing very heavily, we managed to make it to school.   **(1 mark)**

   b. We had a very enjoyable trip to the cinema, after a tasty meal of pizza and salad.   **(1 mark)**

   c. Nick was passionate about football, despite never having been to a big match.   **(1 mark)**

   d. Sarah said we should meet at the shops since it was the easiest option.   **(1 mark)**

   e. Let's go swimming in the morning, unless you have something better to do.   **(1 mark)**

2 Tick the correct box to indicate whether the words in bold are main clauses or subordinate clauses.   **(4 marks)**

Sentence	Main clause	Subordinate clause
Despite the poor turn-out, the performers had a great night.		
Once the children knew the method, **they could solve the word problems**.		
We all rushed down to the shore, although it looked less inviting in the drizzle.		
As the sun began to set, a few people ventured out into the cooler air.		

3 **Tick** the sentence which is grammatically **incorrect**.   **(1 mark)**

   a. When he saw the size of the wolf, Hassan screamed in terror.   ☐

   b. There's no point having breakfast now because it's almost lunchtime.   ☐

   c. As Stella looked out across the sea to the distant horizon.   ☐

   d. In the middle of the night, as all went quiet, I heard a wolf howl.   ☐

Total — 21

1 Underline the **pronouns** in the following sentences.

a. Katie and I unwrapped the sandwich, then quickly ate it. **(1 mark)**

b. They brought Liam to see us last night. **(1 mark)**

c. After Miles had picked some flowers for me, he put them in the kitchen. **(1 mark)**

d. Sipping the smoothie slowly, she was sure it tasted rather odd. **(1 mark)**

2 Rewrite the following paragraph, inserting pronouns where they could replace nouns. **(4 marks)**

Sian and Chloe went to visit their grandma. Their grandma lived in an old, rambling manor by the seaside, covered in twisting ivy and with a front door hanging off its hinges. Approaching the front window, the girls knocked on the front window when they saw Grandma through the murky glass. When Grandma saw the girls Grandma was thrilled and ran outside to hug the girls. Grandma hadn't seen Sian and Chloe for a long time and Grandma asked if the girls would stay a while to help fix up the house and give the house a good clean.

....

....

....

....

....

....

....

Relative pronouns **refer back** to a noun.

Top tip!

3 Tick the correct box to indicate which sentence contains a **relative pronoun**. (1 mark)

a. How many people living in the countryside do you know? ☐

b. We are all fairly sure that our homework is due in today. ☐

c. One of my relatives, who lives by the sea, is moving to the city. ☐

d. I'm not really very hungry, although I could manage a sandwich. ☐

4 Complete these sentences with a relative pronoun.

a. The lady, ... lived in the old cottage, moved
to a new house. (1 mark)

b. The dog, ... owner was quite poorly, was very sad. (1 mark)

c. We had all eaten the vegetable pie, ...
tasted amazing! (1 mark)

d. There are lots of books .... I still haven't read yet. (1 mark)

5 Underline the **possessive pronouns** in the following sentences.

a. I've got all my books but I can't find yours. (1 mark)

b. Becca said the football was hers but Sam was sure it was his. (1 mark)

c. Mum said they were their towels but I knew they were ours. (1 mark)

d. I thought we were all going to my house but I'm happy to go to yours. (1 mark)

6 Tick the correct box to indicate the type of **pronouns** in bold in
each sentence. (2 marks)

Sentence	Possessive	Relative
These shoes are similar to **mine**.		
I have a baby brother **who** is more annoying than yours!		

Total —— 19

Adverbs and adverbials

❶ Say whether the **adverbs** or **adverbials** in bold in these sentences show **how**, **where**, **when** or **how often**.

a. **After a while**, I went home as I had waited **patiently** for
one hour. **(1 mark)**

After a while: ....

patiently: ....

b. **Cautiously**, I crept bit by bit **into the dark depths** of the
gaping cave. **(1 mark)**

Cautiously: ....

into the dark depths: ....

c. **Still** feeling unconfident, Grace **reluctantly** tried the
Maths questions. **(1 mark)**

Still: ....

reluctantly: ....

d. Inching **nervously** forward, the children **frequently** slipped
on the ice. **(1 mark)**

nervously: ....

frequently: ....

❷ Insert an appropriate adverb to say more about the **verbs** in
these sentences.

a. Far out to sea, the armada of ships moved ....
across the horizon. **(1 mark)**

b. Having just won the final, the team jumped ....
in the air. **(1 mark)**

c. ...., the bank robber was not charged,
despite so many witnesses. **(1 mark)**

d. The children were all ....
keen to finish their art. **(1 mark)**

Adverbs describing adjectives

❶ Underline the adverbs that say more about the **adjectives** in the following sentences.

   a. Freddy said the day was completely ruined due to the bad weather. **(1 mark)**

   b. All the children agreed that the fair had been really exciting. **(1 mark)**

   c. Our summer holiday was quite disappointing as there wasn't a lot to do. **(1 mark)**

   d. Our very naughty dog was in trouble for chewing Mum's slippers. **(1 mark)**

Fronted adverbials

❶ Which **two** sentences use a **fronted adverbial** at the start? Tick two boxes. **(2 marks)**

   a. In the far distance, Claire could see a boat sailing on the horizon. ☐

   b. The old man, who only yesterday had been very ill, made a full recovery. ☐

   c. Late last night, we heard heavy footsteps as we walked through the graveyard. ☐

   d. Lucky old Ben, Cara thought, as she waved her friend off to the seaside. ☐

   e. The Head Teacher was liked and respected by all the children. ☐

Adverbs giving more information about other adverbs

❶ Insert **quite**, **very**, **so**, **really** or **rather** before the **adverbs** in these sentences to make them more precise. You can use each word more than once.

   a. Sarah skipped .... quickly to the shore's edge. **(1 mark)**

   b. I was .... terribly excited at the news I almost burst. **(1 mark)**

   c. I screamed when Dan .... nearly lost his footing. **(1 mark)**

   d. After my little sister ate .... too much chocolate, she felt sick. **(1 mark)**

   e. My brother was .... desperately afraid of the dark. **(1 mark)**

   f. As it had started to rain, we went home .... willingly. **(1 mark)**

   g. With most members of staff ill, the Head Teacher .... reluctantly closed the school. **(1 mark)**

Total —— 21

1 Highlight the two **prepositions** that show **place** or **position** in each sentence.

a. Zac hid behind the settee while his sister Sophie sat in the chair. **(1 mark)**

b. Mum found James's socks under the bed, inside his school shoes. **(1 mark)**

c. Monty the dog chased Tabitha the cat round the corner and up the tree. **(1 mark)**

d. We jumped quickly off the wall and hid beneath the oak tree. **(1 mark)**

e. We could make out a spider on the ceiling, crawling away from its web. **(1 mark)**

f. Sam liked to put lettuce in his sandwich before wrapping it in foil. **(1 mark)**

2 Tick the box against the sentence that contains a preposition in a phrase indicating **time**. **(1 mark)**

a. On Tuesdays we go swimming with our friends. ☐

b. The leaves are starting to fall off the trees. ☐

c. Lee and Michael wanted to go to Australia to see kangaroos. ☐

d. The books were piled so high that they were going to topple. ☐

3 Complete the sentences with **prepositions**.

a. My family and I are travelling .... Cornwall .... train. **(1 mark)**

b. High .... in the clear blue sky, the sun shone fiercely. **(1 mark)**

c. Grace and Chloe lifted Benji .... the
garden gate.   **(1 mark)**

d. When I got .... the bus, I put my bag

.... my seat.   **(1 mark)**

4 Write a preposition that can be used with each word.

a. similar ....   **(1 mark)**

b. according ....   **(1 mark)**

c. inspired ....   **(1 mark)**

d. equal ....   **(1 mark)**

e. complain ....   **(1 mark)**

f. interfere ....   **(1 mark)**

g. agree ....   **(1 mark)**

h. rely ....   **(1 mark)**

5 Which pair of prepositions is most suitable for this sentence? Tick one box.

The thief escaped by climbing .... a window and .... a getaway car.   **(1 mark)**

a. into / on ☐

b. onto / through ☐

c. through / into ☐

d. behind / onto ☐

Total $\frac{}{20}$

Grammar Terms | Prepositions   19

1 Underline all the **determiners** in these proverbs.

   a. A bird in the hand is worth two in the bush.   **(1 mark)**

   b. The early bird catches the worm.   **(1 mark)**

   c. The pen is mightier than the sword.   **(1 mark)**

   d. An apple each day keeps the doctor away.   **(1 mark)**

2 Insert an appropriate determiner in the following sentences.

   a. We chatted for hours about ....
   excellent trip.   **(1 mark)**

   b. After .... stressful afternoon, we finally
   sorted it out.   **(1 mark)**

   c. Max put on .... orange t-shirt before
   going out to play.   **(1 mark)**

   d. We had such .... amazing time
   on holiday!   **(1 mark)**

3 Underline the **possessive pronouns** acting as determiners in these sentences.

   a. We had the time of our lives on our most recent holiday
   to Thailand.   **(1 mark)**

   b. Her pile of books fell off the table when she banged into
   it with her bag.   **(1 mark)**

   c. After a long time filling out her passport form, Mum stuck
   it in its envelope and posted it.   **(1 mark)**

   d. They are very enthusiastic about their forthcoming rugby
   celebration.   **(1 mark)**

4 Find all the determiners in each sentence and write them on the answer lines.

a. Our neighbours had had enough of that barking dog! **(2 marks)**

....

....

b. My dad feels strongly about the environment. **(2 marks)**

....

....

c. Our holiday was ruined by the weather. **(2 marks)**

....

....

d. There is just enough of this pizza to go round our group. **(2 marks)**

....

....

Top tip!

Remember, the determiner **an** is always used before a word starting with a vowel.

Total $\frac{}{20}$

1 Give the definition of a **clause**.   (1 mark)

....

2 Tick the box to show whether the words in bold are **clauses**
or **phrases**.   (4 marks)

Sentence	Phrase	Clause
We all breathed **a sigh of relief** when Kir put the ball in the net.		
Full of mischief, **the tiny puppy made his way over to the washing basket**.		
Everyone clapped in delight for the winning team.		
Talia stared **in wonder** at the sight of so much glittering treasure.		

3 Say whether the clauses in bold in these sentences are **main**
or **subordinate**.

a. We all went off to the park **even though it was
   dreadful weather**.   (1 mark)

....

b. **Jack was going skiing for the first time** and was
   feeling rather nervous.   (1 mark)

....

c. **When he looked up from his breakfast**, Rob was
   shocked to see a dinosaur standing there!   (1 mark)

....

d. Erin and Stella, **who had just been on an African safari**,
   were able to talk about lions and tigers.   (1 mark)

....

e. **My walking boots**, which I had just cleaned,
   were once again thick with mud.   (1 mark)

....

4 Join these pairs of sentences to make **two clauses joined by a conjunction**. An example has been done for you.

We went straight out to play.   We hadn't finished our meal.

We went straight out to play, even though we hadn't finished our meal.

a. The blue team was the favourite.   The red team won.   **(1 mark)**

....

b. The children lined up for assembly.   The fire-alarm started ringing.   **(1 mark)**

....

c. Stephanie hadn't been invited to Eva's party.   She decided to turn up with a gift.   **(1 mark)**

....

d. You should take the dog for a walk.   I took him out last time.   **(1 mark)**

....

e. I put the cat out in the garden.   She always comes straight back in.   **(1 mark)**

....

Remember! A main clause makes sense on its own; a subordinate clause doesn't.

Top tip!

Total $\frac{}{15}$

1 Underline the **relative clauses** in the following sentences.

a. The old lady, who I met yesterday on the beach, has called round with flowers. **(1 mark)**

b. After our lunch we went to the cinema, which was in a nearby shopping complex. **(1 mark)**

c. Sarim and Sophie, whose parents were on holiday, stayed with us for the weekend. **(1 mark)**

d. My dad's car, which had only just been repaired, broke down on the motorway. **(1 mark)**

e. Finally we have won a match, which might come as a complete surprise to you! **(1 mark)**

f. The bakery that we use is on the corner. **(1 mark)**

2 Circle the **incorrect relative pronoun** in these sentences. Write the correct relative pronoun in the answer space.

a. I thanked the old man next door which feeds my cat when we are away. **(1 mark)**

....

b. My sister that has just returned from her school trip has come home very tired and grumpy. **(1 mark)**

....

c. Our neighbour, who garden shed was broken into, reported it to the police. **(1 mark)**

....

d. Those books, who we've all read, can go to the charity shop. **(1 mark)**

....

3 Insert a suitable **relative pronoun** in the sentences below.

a. We have been lucky with the weather, ... was rather grim yesterday.

(1 mark)

b. I searched for the book in the library .... we had tried to find in the bookshop.

(1 mark)

c. My best friend, ... is moving house next month, is packing up already.

(1 mark)

d. I can't believe that our supper, ... we put in the oven ages ago, still isn't ready!

(1 mark)

4 Rewrite these sentences using **relative pronouns**.
An example has been done for you.

Cerys's books, scattered untidily on the table, were all mystery stories.
Cerys's books, which were scattered untidily on the table, were all mystery stories.

a. My mum, a former Olympic swimming champion, took us to the local pool.

(1 mark)

....

b. Our school grounds, recently damaged in a flood, now look better than ever.

(1 mark)

....

c. Max, eager to win some medals, won the 100 metre race and the hurdles. **(1 mark)**

....

The relative pronoun **whose** can't be omitted.
For example:
The cat, whose owner was away, stayed at a neighbour's.

But others can be omitted:
The cat, who was sitting on the wall, purred softly.
The cat, sitting on the wall, purred softly.

Top tip!

Total $\frac{}{17}$

1 Write two examples of a **statement**.

a. .... (1 mark)

b. .... (1 mark)

2 Write two examples of a **question**.

a. .... (1 mark)

b. .... (1 mark)

3 Write two examples of a **command**.

a. .... (1 mark)

b. .... (1 mark)

4 Write two examples of an **exclamation**.

a. .... (1 mark)

b. .... (1 mark)

Top tip! It makes sense that an exclamation mark comes at the end of an exclamation and a question mark at the end of a question! Often an exclamation mark comes at the end of a command too.

5 Use **command verbs** to complete these sentences.

a. .... your breakfast immediately! (1 mark)

b. .... at the pedestrian crossing and

.... both ways before you cross. (1 mark)

c. .... your homework then

.... it to your teacher. (1 mark)

d. .... a thank-you note to your friends

who bought you presents. (1 mark)

6 Tick the correct box to indicate the sentence type. **(4 marks)**

Sentence	Statement	Question	Command	Exclamation
Take the first road on the left, then turn left.				
How many more days until the holidays?				
I've just been bitten by a snake!				
It's a perfect day for a picnic.				

7 Write questions that would match these answers.

a. ....

.... **(1 mark)**

There are approximately 250 children, aged 4–11.

b. ....

.... **(1 mark)**

We went to Europe for two weeks and had a weekend in Scotland.

c. ....

.... **(1 mark)**

Turn right at the end of the road, then first left after the post office.

Total $\frac{}{19}$

1 Underline the **subjects** of the following sentences.

a. Finn watched the netball match. **(1 mark)**

b. Last week, my friends and I took the bus home.   **(1 mark)**

c. After a while, Sasha stopped talking and listened to the teacher.   **(1 mark)**

d. The rain lashed continuously all through the night.   **(1 mark)**

e. Whenever we can, my sisters and I help our mum with the washing-up.   **(1 mark)**

f. You have eaten all the chocolates!   **(1 mark)**

2 Tick the sentence where the verb **does not agree** with the subject. Then write the sentence correctly in the space.   **(1 mark)**

a. My parents aren't always in agreement about how long I should spend on homework.   ☐

b. Aisha and Will doesn't have packed lunches with them today.   ☐

c. The herd of elephants is charging swiftly through the jungle.   ☐

d. Saskia and I are in trouble for not listening more carefully.   ☐

....

3 Write the verbs **to be** and **to go** in the past tense in the tables.

a.

to be			
I	....	we	....
you	....	you	....
he / she / it	....	they	....

(3 marks)

b.

to go			
I	....	we	....
you	....	you	....
he / she / it	....	they	....

(3 marks)

4 Choose the correct form of the verbs in brackets to agree with the subjects in the following sentences.

a. We (**to walk**) towards the cliff edge, taking care that the wind didn't (**to blow**) our hats off.

(1 mark)

....

b. As you (**to discover**), the water (**to be**) very deep in the harbour.

(1 mark)

....

c. She (**to take**) great care when (**to draw**) diagrams and (**to use**) a very sharp nib.

(1 mark)

....

d. At 6 o'clock in the morning, (**to be**) it any wonder I (**to be**) too tired to eat?

(1 mark)

....

e. Sol (**to run**) over the finish line then (**to throw**) himself on the ground in relief.

(1 mark)

....

f. We often (**to watch**) animated films on TV but they (**to be**) much better at the cinema.

(1 mark)

....

Total $\frac{}{19}$

❶ Underline the **subject** and **circle** the **object** in the following sentences.

    a. My parents love watching the football.   **(1 mark)**

    b. A wasp has just stung me.   **(1 mark)**

    c. The three children pushed the garden gate.   **(1 mark)**

    d. The policeman arrested the thief.   **(1 mark)**

    e. The horses were eating hay.   **(1 mark)**

    f. My meddling little brother has broken my computer.   **(1 mark)**

❷ Write sentences containing an appropriate subject and object for these verbs.

    a. to eat   **(1 mark)**

    ....

    b. to carry   **(1 mark)**

    ....

    c. to bite   **(1 mark)**

    ....

    d. to marry   **(1 mark)**

    ....

    e to play   **(1 mark)**

    ....

    f. to read   **(1 mark)**

    ....

3 Which sentence below does not contain an object? Tick one box. **(1 mark)**

a. There are ten girls skipping. ☐

b. We are eating our supper. ☐

c. I've just got to school. ☐

d. Here are the books I've just read. ☐

4 Add an object to expand these simple sentences.
An example has been done for you.

The choir sang very well.
The choir sang the songs very well.

a. My mum likes baking. **(1 mark)**

....

b. Do you like drawing? **(1 mark)**

....

c. My sister is great at riding. **(1 mark)**

....

d. We've all been playing. **(1 mark)**

....

Remember to look at the verb in a sentence then ask the question, **what or who is it acting on?** The answer will tell you what the object is, if there is one.

Top tip!

Total 17

1 Write two sentences in the **active voice**.

a. .... (1 mark)

b. .... (1 mark)

2 Write two sentences in the **passive voice**.

a. .... (1 mark)

b. .... (1 mark)

3 Turn these sentences from the **active** to the **passive voice**.

a. The children's parents took them to the disco for
the Year 6 treat. (1 mark)

....

....

b. Sir Edmund Hillary and Sherpa Tenzing conquered
Everest in 1953. (1 mark)

....

....

c. The cooks burned the apple pie because the oven
was too hot. (1 mark)

....

....

d. When the bin started to overflow, Millie threw out
the rubbish. (1 mark)

....

....

e. The dentist extracted my big sister's tooth. (1 mark)

....

....

f. Finally, the determined junior team won the champion's cup.

(1 mark)

....

....

4 Tick the correct box to show whether the following sentences are in the **active voice** or the **passive voice**.

Sentence	Active voice	Passive voice
The angry wasps stung the children.		
My mother brought my friends and me to the cinema.		
A family was rescued from the blaze by a fireman.		
We were given an ultimatum by our teacher.		
The thieves were being pursued.		
We left our picnic blanket by the edge of the river.		

(6 marks)

5 Turn these sentences from the passive voice into the active voice.

a. My energetic dog was walked all week by an enthusiastic dog-walker. **(1 mark)**

....

....

b. The transatlantic race was completed by the team in record time. **(1 mark)**

....

....

c. Three phone calls were received by the emergency team last night. **(1 mark)**

....

....

d. The newspaper article written by the young journalist was fascinating. **(1 mark)**

....

....

Total $\frac{}{20}$

❶ Underline the **direct speech** in the following passage.   **(3 marks)**

When Benji heard the thunder in the middle of the night, he said it

was the loudest noise he'd ever heard. "Make it go away!" he shouted.

His mum said that it couldn't hurt him and it might help to count the

seconds between the thunder claps and the lightning bolts.

"It's nature, sweetheart, and it won't last forever," she reassured him.

"Come, on let's count together."

"One, two, three, four…," they counted. By eight, Benji was

already asleep.

❷ The following sentences are examples of direct speech but all the punctuation has been left out.

Rewrite the sentences and insert **all** the missing punctuation in the correct places.
An example has been done for you.

We really should visit Grandma this afternoon said Mum
"We really should visit Grandma this afternoon," said Mum.

a. I would really like to go to the cinema to see that new
Spiderman film Paul said   **(1 mark)**

....

....

b. We knew that eventually we would move to America the
children told their neighbours   **(1 mark)**

....

....

....

Top tip!

Use a range of different words for **said** to make your writing more interesting.

c. Start running now Jack screamed (1 mark)

....

d. Taylor said I hope I remembered to put the chocolate brownies
in the picnic basket (1 mark)

....

....

e. Have you brought your library book in today asked the librarian (1 mark)

....

3 Rewrite these sentences using inverted commas to show direct speech. Change the
other punctuation if necessary.

a. Max asked Billy if he would play football with him. (1 mark)

....

b. Harry announced that everyone could come to his house for tea. (1 mark)

....

c. All the Year 6 spectators shouted to the lacrosse team to score. (1 mark)

....

d. Honor asked her teacher if she could have some extra time in the
reading test. (1 mark)

....

4 How many words to replace **said** when using direct speech can
you think of? Write them below. **(up to 10 marks)**

....	....	....	....	....
....	....	....	....	....

Vary your writing by using
a mixture of direct speech
and reported speech.

Top tip!

Total $\frac{}{22}$

1 a. Explain some of the differences between **informal** and **formal** speech and writing. **(2 marks)**

....

b. When might you use each type? ....

.... **(2 marks)**

2 Would you use **informal** or **formal** writing for the following?

a. A text to your friend. .... **(1 mark)**

b. A letter to the Head Teacher. .... **(1 mark)**

c. A postcard to your mum and dad. .... **(1 mark)**

d. A letter to an author whose book you liked.

.... **(1 mark)**

e. Your diary. .... **(1 mark)**

f. An email to your close friends. .... **(1 mark)**

g. Your speech for a public speaking competition.

.... **(1 mark)**

3 Write two diary entries for a recent weekend, using the appropriate type of language for this genre. **(4 marks)**

Saturday
....
....
....
....

Sunday
....
....
....
....

4 Insert the **subjunctive** form of the verb **to be** to complete these sentences. **(2 marks)**

a. Her Majesty requires that all visitors .... respectful of the palace grounds.

b. If only we .... able to join you on holiday!

5 You are introducing your favourite author in assembly who is visiting your school to talk about his / her book.
Write a short speech welcoming him / her and giving some background information about them and their latest book. **(4 marks)**

....

....

....

....

....

....

....

6 Rewrite the following sentences using **Standard English**.

a. We ain't gonna go to the park 'coz we's got visitors. **(1 mark)**

....

b. Pick them books up now else I'll be proper cross. **(1 mark)**

....

c. She would of helped youse if youse would of asked. **(1 mark)**

....

d. I don't want no chips with me chicken. **(1 mark)**

....

....

Total $\frac{}{25}$

1 Why do we use **punctuation marks**? **(1 mark)**

to Show if your speaching or loudly or quiety.

2 When do we use **capital letters** and **full stops**? **(1 mark)**

to shaw start and finish sentence

3 Insert **capital letters** and **full stops** into the following passage so that it makes sense. **(4 marks)**

when Maggie and Jack reached the outskirts of london they were quite overwhelmed at the sight of some of the iconic buildings looming before them. Were the houses of Parliament, then Big Ben, next Westminster Abbey and st Paul's cathedral. Taking a boat on the river thames, the children were wide-eyed in awe and amazement as they saw the city from a different perspective. All they could think about was how impressed their teacher, Mrs Muggins, would be when they went in to school on Monday morning

4 Only one of the sentences below is correctly punctuated. Tick the box to indicate which one. **(1 mark)**

Sentence	Correct?
My brother said his friend pat was going to watch the first star wars film with him.	✓
At breezybank primary school, the best teachers, in my opinion, are mrs mason and mr burns.	
after a long wait in London, the children got on the bus to Cambridge and went home.	
My next adventure will be to take a raft down the River Ganges in India.	
Every wednesday, I go to the swimming baths with Claire and Sam.	

Capital letters are not joined to the next letter – they stand alone and should be twice the height of short letters such as **a** or **o**.

Top tip!

5 Rewrite the following sentences, correcting any missing or wrongly placed **capital letters** and **full stops**.

a. "I'm off to the Shops. now," said bill to his Sister. "there's a special Discount on at sweetsavers" **(1 mark)**

"I'm off to the Shops Now", said Bill to his Sister. "Theres a special discount on sweetsavers"

b. we couldn't understand how maddie had forgotten her Homework for the second time in a Week our teacher had told her many Times **(1 mark)**

We couldn't understand how Maddie had forgotten her homework for the second time in a week. Our teacher had told her many times

c. looking out of the window tom was struggling. to see his dad's volvo through the. fog then it started to clear and before he knew it tom was outside playing. in the Sunshine **(1 mark)**

Looking out of the window tom was struglin g. To see his dads volvo through the. fog theny it started to clear and before he new it tom was outsi playing. (in the Sunshine)

d. megan and amy were off to paris to visit the eiffel tower. which they hoped to climb to the Top they were going with their Cousin arthur who spoke french fluently **(1 mark)**

megan and amy were off to paris to visit the eiffel tower which they hoped to climb to the top aft they were going with their cousins author who spoke french fluntly

e. I watched the lion king when we went to London it was truly amazing and probably the best performance I've ever seen I would actually go back and watch it again **(1 mark)**

I watched the lion king when we went to london it was truly amazing and probable the best peforma I have ever seen I would actually go back and watch it again

When I write, I remember to make capital letters tall. I do not join them.

Total
12

1 When do we use **question marks**? **(1 mark)**

....

2 When do we use **exclamation marks**? **(1 mark)**

....

3 Add either a **question mark** or an **exclamation mark** to these sentences.

a. It really was the most dreadful weather.......... **(1 mark)**

b. "I'm going home now, aren't you.........." **(1 mark)**

c. "There's not much point in staying any longer, is there.........." **(1 mark)**

d. "Wow.......... Look at the flooding further down the river bank.......... **(2 marks)**

e. Had they really arrived that morning in glorious sunshine..........

(1 mark)

4 Write suitable questions for these answers.

a. .... **(1 mark)**

He had white hair, round glasses and was a little stooped.

b. .... **(1 mark)**

Three girls, two boys and a small, yappy dog.

c. .... **(1 mark)**

I cooked it according to the recipe.

d. .... **(1 mark)**

Every day of the week except Sundays.

GRAMMAR TERMS

Nouns

pages 4–5

Nouns

1 a. We ate the <u>pizza</u> and drank our <u>juice</u>.
(1 mark)

b. <u>She</u> swapped her <u>book</u> at the <u>library</u>.
(1 mark)

c. <u>He</u> dropped lots of <u>pencils</u> on the <u>floor</u>.
(1 mark)

d. The <u>girls</u> stopped talking and listened to their <u>teacher</u>. **(1 mark)**

e. Our <u>school</u> closed early because of the heavy <u>snow</u>. **(1 mark)**

f. <u>Scarves</u>, <u>gloves</u> and <u>hats</u> – all were packed for the <u>trip</u>. **(1 mark)**

Noun types

1 They either start with a capital letter because they are at the beginning of the sentence or they are proper nouns. **(1 mark)**

2 a. The <u>ducks</u> wandered down the <u>road</u> and into the <u>field</u>. **(1 mark)**

b. Our <u>team</u> finished early on <u>Wednesday</u> because of the <u>snow</u>. **(1 mark)**

c. <u>Phil</u> showed great <u>courage</u> when faced with the <u>tiger</u>. **(1 mark)**

d. <u>Prince William</u> visited <u>Wales</u> at the beginning of <u>July</u>. **(1 mark)**

e. My <u>football</u> hit the top <u>bar</u> of the <u>net</u>.
(1 mark)

f. We went in the <u>sea</u>, although the <u>weather</u> was grim and the <u>waves</u> rough. **(1 mark)**

Expanded noun phrases

1 a. <u>The beautiful blue butterfly</u> landed on <u>my bare shoulder</u>. **(1 mark)**

b. We showed <u>a lot of courage</u> in spite of <u>the awful danger</u> we were in. **(1 mark)**

c. <u>My old grandfather</u> kept <u>two herds of cows</u> on <u>his five-acre farm</u>. **(1 mark)**

d. <u>Our local primary school</u> has <u>a well-stocked library</u> full of <u>interesting books</u>.
(1 mark)

e. Sasha went to <u>the beautiful islands</u> of Guernsey and Jersey for <u>his first-ever holiday</u>. **(1 mark)**

f. After eating <u>cheese and ham sandwiches</u>, <u>my little sister</u> and I headed home. **(1 mark)**

2 Answers will vary. Examples:

countryside	The never-ending countryside
determination	His relentless determination
disgust	My utter disgust
ocean	The vast ocean
swarm	A dense swarm of bees

(5 marks)

Verbs

pages 6–7

Identifying verbs

1 a. The fire <u>roared</u> in the dark night sky.
(1 mark)

b. We <u>left</u> our towels on the beach.
(1 mark)

c. The soldiers <u>fire</u> at the practice target.
(1 mark)

d. The aim of the game is to <u>aim</u> high.
(1 mark)

e. Somehow we always <u>manage</u> to <u>forget</u> someone! **(1 mark)**

f. When you have <u>finished</u>, <u>start</u> the next task. **(1 mark)**

Past and present tense

1

Verb	Present	Past
to eat	I am eating/ I eat	I ate/I was eating
to be	I am being/ I am	I was/I was being
to know	I know	I knew
to go	I am going/ I go	I went/I was going
to admit	I am admitting/ I admit	I admitted/I was admitting

(5 marks)

2 a. go: present   were: past   **(1 mark)**
b. barks: present   are: present   **(1 mark)**
c. see: present   was: past   **(1 mark)**

3 a. We were enjoying the performance tremendously. **(1 mark)**

b. The bright sun was shining high in the clear blue sky. **(1 mark)**

Future tense

1 a. we shall/will go swimming
OR   we shall/will swim **(1 mark)**

b. I will/shall be sailing
   OR   I shall/will sail   **(1 mark)**

c. the children shall/will be celebrating
   OR   the children shall/will celebrate   **(1 mark)**

d. we shall/will be wearing
   OR   we shall/will wear   **(1 mark)**

Modal verbs
pages 8–9
Modals indicating possibility

1 a. We (may) be going away next week but there's a chance Dad (may) not be able to come.   **(1 mark)**

b. Jon (may) play football this Saturday and if he does, he (could) be made team captain.   **(1 mark)**

c. There (can) be as many as fifty children in the pool at any given time; there (could) even be more   **(1 mark)**

d. Joseph thought there (might) be heavy traffic so he asked if he (could) walk to school.   **(1 mark)**

2 Answers may vary. Examples:
a. I may go to the shops later; I haven't made my mind up yet.   **(1 mark)**

b. If the weather stays uncertain, we may need to bring our waterproofs.   **(1 mark)**

c. It may not be possible to change our plans about going to the cinema.   **(1 mark)**

d. It might snow later according to the weather forecast.   **(1 mark)**

3 b. Might you be coming to our house later? ✓   **(1 mark)**

Adverbs to indicate possibility

1 a. We clearly aren't going to get there on time with this heavy traffic.   **(1 mark)**

b. It's obviously the rush hour since it's 5 o'clock.   **(1 mark)**

c. I certainly won't be coming at this time again.   **(1 mark)**

d. Maybe we should have taken the country roads.   **(1 mark)**

2 Answers will vary. Examples:
a. You definitely have to eat more healthily.   **(1 mark)**

b. Sarim obviously isn't going to come now.   **(1 mark)**

c. Surely the shop is closed at this time of night.   **(1 mark)**

d. Erin clearly has more homework to finish.   **(1 mark)**

3

Adverb	Certainty	Uncertainty
unlikely		✓
possibly		✓
definitely	✓	
clearly	✓	
perhaps		✓

(5 marks)

Adjectives
pages 10–11
Adjectives

1 a. Freddy, that naughty boy in Year 2, was in big trouble yet again.   **(1 mark)**

b. With his new football in his hands, Archie headed towards the muddy field.   **(1 mark)**

c. Although Brogan was nervous about the test, he was nonetheless a determined boy.   **(1 mark)**

d. Despite the atrocious weather conditions, the well-known team of explorers set off.   **(1 mark)**

2 Answers will vary. Examples:
a. The **furry** cat slept on the **grubby** mat.   **(1 mark)**

b. My **annoying** sister came in and sat on the **comfiest** armchair.   **(1 mark)**

c. My **wonderful** mum cooked our **favourite** dinner.   **(1 mark)**

d. We came across a **vast** field full of **beautiful** flowers.   **(1 mark)**

Adjectives comparing two nouns

1 a. Matt is older than Thomas.   **(1 mark)**

b. Freya's hair is curlier than her big sister's.   **(1 mark)**

c. I think the countryside is more / less beautiful than inner-city areas.   **(1 mark)**

d. Our homework was more / less interesting this week than last week.   **(1 mark)**

Adjectives comparing more than two nouns

1 a. Mia had the longest hair of all the girls in her class.   **(1 mark)**

b. That actress had to be the most / least fascinating person I'd ever interviewed.   **(1 mark)**

c. We had the most / least intelligent people on our quiz team.   **(1 mark)**

d. It was the most disgusting meal we'd ever eaten.   **(1 mark)**

Conjunctions

pages 12–13

Conjunctions that join two clauses of equal importance

1 a. My mother likes to go to Spain on holiday <u>but</u> my father prefers France. **(1 mark)**

b. We couldn't make swimming tonight <u>for</u> our car wouldn't start. **(1 mark)**

c. I find long division really easy <u>yet</u> long multiplication really hard! **(1 mark)**

d. It was way past our bedtime <u>so</u> our parents sent us to bed. **(1 mark)**

e. We grabbed our swimsuits <u>and</u> set off for the swimming pool. **(1 mark)**

f. Kathy hadn't a clue where the map was, <u>nor</u> did she really care. **(1 mark)**

2 a. Milo has a dog <u>but</u> he hasn't got a cat. **(1 mark)**

b. Seb likes carrots <u>and</u> he likes cabbage. **(1 mark)**

c. My sister is extremely tall <u>but / yet</u> I am exceptionally short. **(1 mark)**

d. Millie is amazing at tennis <u>but / yet</u> she struggles with badminton. **(1 mark)**

e. The rain was very heavy <u>so</u> the children couldn't play football. **(1 mark)**

Conjunctions that join a main clause to a subordinate clause

1 a. <u>Although</u> it was snowing very heavily, we managed to make it to school. **(1 mark)**

b. We had a very enjoyable trip to the cinema, <u>after</u> a tasty meal of pizza and salad. **(1 mark)**

c. Nick was passionate about football, <u>despite</u> never having been to a big match. **(1 mark)**

d. Sarah said we should meet at the shops <u>since</u> it was the easiest option. **(1 mark)**

e. Let's go swimming in the morning, <u>unless</u> you have something better to do. **(1 mark)**

2

Sentence	Main clause	Subordinate clause
Despite the poor turn-out, the performers had a great night.		✓
Once the children knew the method, **they could solve the word problems**.	✓	
We all rushed down to the shore, although it looked less inviting in the drizzle.	✓	
As the sun began to set, a few people ventured out into the cooler air.		✓

(4 marks)

3 c. As Stella looked out across the sea to the distant horizon. ✓ **(1 mark)**

Pronouns

pages 14–15

1 a. Katie and <u>I</u> unwrapped the sandwich, then quickly ate <u>it</u>. **(1 mark)**

b. <u>They</u> brought Liam to see <u>us</u> last night. **(1 mark)**

c. After Miles had picked some flowers for <u>me</u>, <u>he</u> put <u>them</u> in the kitchen. **(1 mark)**

d. Sipping the smoothie slowly, <u>she</u> was sure <u>it</u> tasted rather odd. **(1 mark)**

2 Sian and Chloe went to visit their grandma. **She** lived in an old, rambling manor by the seaside, covered in twisting ivy and with a front door hanging off its hinges. Approaching the front window, the girls knocked on **it** when **they** saw Grandma through the murky glass. When **she** saw **them**, Grandma was thrilled and ran outside to hug **them**. **She** hadn't seen **them** for a long time and **she** asked if **they** would stay a while to help fix up the house and give **it** a good clean. **(4 marks)**

3 c. One of my relatives, who lives by the sea, is moving to the city. ✓ **(1 mark)**

4 a. The lady, <u>who</u> lived in the old cottage, moved to new house. **(1 mark)**

b. The dog, <u>whose</u> owner was quite poorly, was very sad. **(1 mark)**

c. We had all eaten the vegetable pie, <u>that/which</u> tasted amazing! **(1 mark)**

d. There are lots of books <u>that/which</u> I still haven't read yet. **(1 mark)**

5 a. I've got all my books but I can't find <u>yours</u>. **(1 mark)**

b. Becca said the football was <u>hers</u> but Sam was sure it was <u>his</u>. **(1 mark)**

c. Mum said they were their towels but I knew they were <u>ours</u>. **(1 mark)**

d. I thought we were all going to my house but I'm happy to go to <u>yours</u>. **(1 mark)**

6

Sentence	Possessive	Relative
These shoes are similar to **mine**.	✓	
I have a baby brother **who** is more annoying than yours!		✓

(2 marks)

Adverbs and adverbials

pages 16–17

Adverbs and adverbials

1 a. After a while: <u>when</u>; patiently: <u>how</u> **(1 mark)**

b. Cautiously: <u>how</u>; into the dark depths: <u>where</u> **(1 mark)**

c. Still: <u>when</u>; reluctantly: <u>how</u> **(1 mark)**
d. nervously: <u>how</u>; frequently: <u>how often</u>
(1 mark)

2 Answers will vary. Examples:
a. Far out to sea, the armada of ships moved **elegantly/swiftly** across the horizon. **(1 mark)**
b. Having just won the final, the team jumped **joyfully/enthusiastically** in the air. **(1 mark)**
c. **Incredibly/unbelievably**, the bank robber was not charged, despite so many witnesses. **(1 mark)**
d. The children were all **desperately/incredibly** keen to finish their art.
(1 mark)

Adverbs describing adjectives
1 a. Freddy said the day was <u>completely</u> ruined due to the bad weather. **(1 mark)**
b. All the children agreed that the fair had been <u>really</u> exciting. **(1 mark)**
c. Our summer holiday was <u>quite</u> disappointing as there wasn't a lot to do. **(1 mark)**
d. Our <u>very</u> naughty dog was in trouble for chewing Mum's slippers. **(1 mark)**

Fronted adverbials
1 a. In the far distance, Claire could see a boat sailing on the horizon. ☑ **(1 mark)**
c. Late last night, we heard heavy footsteps as we walked through the graveyard. ☑ **(1 mark)**

Adverbs giving more information about other adverbs
1 a. Sarah skipped <u>quite/very/really/rather</u> quickly to the shore's edge. **(1 mark)**
b. I was <u>so</u> terribly excited at the news I almost burst. **(1 mark)**
c. I screamed when Dan <u>very/so</u> nearly lost his footing. **(1 mark)**
d. After my little sister ate <u>rather</u> too much chocolate she felt sick. **(1 mark)**
e. My brother was <u>quite/very/so/really/rather</u> desperately afraid of the dark. **(1 mark)**
f. As it had started to rain, we went home <u>quite/really/very/rather</u> willingly.
(1 mark)
g. With most members of staff ill, the Head Teacher <u>rather/really/very</u> reluctantly closed the school. **(1 mark)**

Prepositions
pages 18–19
1. a. Zac hid **behind** the settee while his sister Sophie sat **in** the chair. **(1 mark)**
b. Mum found James's socks **under** the bed **inside** his school shoes. **(1 mark)**
c. Monty the dog chased Tabitha the cat **round** the corner and **up** the tree.
(1 mark)
d. We jumped quickly **off** the wall and hid **beneath** the oak tree. **(1 mark)**
e. We could make out a spider **on** the ceiling crawling **away from** its web.
(1 mark)
f. Sam liked to put lettuce **in** his sandwich before wrapping it **in** foil. **(1 mark)**

2 a. On Tuesdays we go swimming with our friends. ☑ **(1 mark)**

3 a. My family and I are travelling **to / around** Cornwall **by** train. **(1 mark)**
b. High **above / up** in the clear blue sky, the sun shone fiercely. **(1 mark)**
c. Grace and Chloe lifted Benji **over** the garden gate. **(1 mark)**
d. When I got **on** the bus, I put my bag **under** / **on** my seat. **(1 mark)**

4 a. similar <u>to</u> **(1 mark)**
b. according <u>to</u> **(1 mark)**
c. inspired <u>by</u> **(1 mark)**
d. equal <u>to</u> **(1 mark)**
e. complain <u>about</u> **(1 mark)**
f. interfere <u>with</u> **(1 mark)**
g. agree <u>with / to</u> **(1 mark)**
h. rely <u>on</u> **(1 mark)**

5 c. through / into ☑ **(1 mark)**

Determiners
pages 20–21
1 a. <u>A</u> bird in <u>the</u> hand is worth two in <u>the</u> bush. **(1 mark)**
b. <u>The</u> early bird catches <u>the</u> worm. **(1 mark)**
c. <u>The</u> pen is mightier than <u>the</u> sword.
(1 mark)
d. <u>An</u> apple <u>each</u> day keeps <u>the</u> doctor away. **(1 mark)**

2 a. We chatted for hours about **the** excellent trip. **(1 mark)**
b. After **a** stressful afternoon, we finally sorted it out. **(1 mark)**
c. Max put on **an** orange t-shirt before going out to play. **(1 mark)**
d. We had such **an** amazing time on holiday! **(1 mark)**

3   **a.** We had the time of our lives on our most recent
 holiday to Thailand. **(1 mark)**
   b. Her pile of books fell off the table when she
 banged into it with her bag. **(1 mark)**
   c. After a long time filling out her passport form, Mum
 stuck it in its envelope and posted it. **(1 mark)**
   d. They are very enthusiastic about their forthcoming
 rugby celebration. **(1 mark)**

4   **a.** our, that **(2 marks)**
   b. My, the **(2 marks)**
   c. Our, the **(2 marks)**
   d. this, our **(2 marks)**

CREATING SENTENCES

Phrases and clauses
pages 22–23

1   A clause contains a verb and can make sense
 as a sentence. **(1 mark)**

2

Sentence	Phrase	Clause
We all breathed **a sigh of relief** when Kir put the ball in the net.	✓	
Full of mischief, **the tiny puppy made his way over to the washing basket**.		✓
Everyone clapped in delight for the winning team.		✓
Talia stared **in wonder** at the sight of so much glittering treasure.	✓	

(4 marks)

3   **a.** subordinate clause **(1 mark)**
   b. main clause **(1 mark)**
   c. subordinate clause **(1 mark)**
   d. subordinate clause **(1 mark)**
   e. main clause **(1 mark)**

4   Answers may vary. Examples:
   a. The blue team was the favourite, however, / but
 the red team won. **(1 mark)**
   b. The children lined up for assembly as / when
 the fire-alarm started ringing. **(1 mark)**
   c. Stephanie hadn't been invited to Eva's party, but
 she decided to turn up with a gift. **(1 mark)**
   d. You can take the dog for a walk because / since
 I took him out last time. **(1 mark)**
   e. I put the cat out in the garden, although /
 even though she always comes straight
 back in. **(1 mark)**

Relative clauses
pages 24–25

1   **a.** The old lady, who I met yesterday on the beach,
 has called round with flowers. **(1 mark)**

   b. After our lunch we went to the cinema, which was
 in a nearby shopping complex. **(1 mark)**
   c. Sarim and Sophie, whose parents were on holiday,
 stayed with us for the weekend. **(1 mark)**
   d. My dad's car, which had only just been repaired,
 broke down on the motorway. **(1 mark)**
   e. Finally we have won a match, which might come
 as a complete surprise to you! **(1 mark)**
   f. The bakery that we use is on the corner. **(1 mark)**

2   **a.** I thanked the old man next door who feeds my cat
 when we are away. **(1 mark)**
   b. My sister who has just returned from her
 school trip has come home very tired
 and grumpy. **(1 mark)**
   c. Our neighbour, whose garden shed was broken
 into, reported it to the police. **(1 mark)**
   d. Those books, which / that we've all read, can go to
 the charity shop. **(1 mark)**

3   **a.** We have been lucky with the weather which was
 rather grim yesterday. **(1 mark)**
   b. I searched for the book in the library which / that
 we had tried to find in the bookshop. **(1 mark)**
   c. My best friend, who is moving house next month,
 is packing up already. **(1 mark)**
   d. I can't believe that our supper, which we put in the
 oven ages ago, still isn't ready! **(1 mark)**

4   **a.** My mum, **who is** a former Olympic swimming
 champion, took us to the local pool. **(1 mark)**
   b. Our school grounds, **which were** recently
 damaged in a flood, now look better than ever.
 (1 mark)
   c. Max, **who was** eager to win some medals, won the
 100 metre race and the hurdles. **(1 mark)**

Sentence types
pages 26–27

1   Accept any two appropriate statements. **(2 marks)**
2   Accept any two appropriate questions. **(2 marks)**
3   Accept any two appropriate commands. **(2 marks)**
4   Accept any two appropriate exclamations. **(2 marks)**
5   Answers will vary. Examples:
   a. Eat / finish your breakfast immediately!
 (1 mark)
   b. Stop / stand at the pedestrian crossing
 and look both ways before you cross.
 (1 mark)
   c. Finish / do your homework then give it to
 your teacher. **(1 mark)**
   d. Write / send a thank-you note to your friends who
 bought you presents.
 (1 mark)

6

Sentence	Statement	Question	Command	Exclamation
Take the first road on the left, then turn left.			✓	
How many more days until the holidays?		✓		
I've just been bitten by a snake!				✓
It's a perfect day for a picnic.	✓			

(4 marks)

7 Answers will vary. Examples:
   a. How many children are there in your
      school? **(1 mark)**
   b. Where did you go on holiday last
      summer? **(1 mark)**
   c. Which way is the train station? **(1 mark)**

SENTENCE FEATURES

Subject–Verb agreement
pages 28–29

1 **a.** <u>Finn</u> watched the netball match. **(1 mark)**
   b. Last week, <u>my friends and I</u> took the
      bus home. **(1 mark)**
   c. After a while, <u>Sasha</u> stopped talking
      and listened to the teacher. **(1 mark)**
   d. <u>The rain</u> lashed continuously all through
      the night. **(1 mark)**
   e. Whenever <u>we</u> can, <u>my sisters and I</u> help
      our mum with the washing-up. **(1 mark)**
   f. <u>You</u> have eaten all the chocolates!
      (1 mark)

2 **b.** Aisha and Will doesn't have packed
      lunches with them today. ✓
      <u>Aisha and Will do not have packed</u>
      <u>lunches with them today.</u> **(1 mark)**

3 a.

to be				
I	**was**	we	**were**	
you	**were**	you	**were**	
he / she / it	**was**	they	**were**	

(3 marks)

b.

to go	
I	**went/<u>was going</u>**
you	**went/<u>were going</u>**
he / she / it	**went/<u>was going</u>**
we	**went/<u>were going</u>**
you	**went/<u>were going</u>**
they	**went/<u>were going</u>**

(3 marks)

4 **a.** We <u>walked</u> towards the cliff edge, taking
      care that the wind didn't <u>blow</u> our hats
      off. **(1 mark)**

   b. As you <u>discovered / will discover</u>, the water
      <u>is / was</u> very deep in the harbour. **(1 mark)**
   c. She <u>takes / took</u> great care when
      <u>drawing</u> diagrams and <u>uses/used</u>
      a very sharp nib. **(1 mark)**
   d. At 6 o'clock in the morning, <u>is/was</u>
      it any wonder I <u>am/was</u> too tired
      to eat? **(1 mark)**
   e. Sol <u>ran/runs</u> over the finish line then
      <u>threw/throws</u> himself on the ground
      in relief. **(1 mark)**
   f. We often <u>watch/watched</u> animated
      films on TV but they <u>are/were</u> much
      better at the cinema. **(1 mark)**

Subject and object
pages 30–31

1 **a.** <u>My parents</u> love watching (the football)
      (1 mark)
   b. <u>A wasp</u> has just stung (me) **(1 mark)**
   c. <u>The three children</u> pushed
      (the garden gate) **(1 mark)**
   d. <u>The policeman</u> arrested (the thief)
      (1 mark)
   e. <u>The horses</u> were eating (hay) **(1 mark)**
   f. <u>My meddling little brother</u> has
      broken (my computer) **(1 mark)**

2 Accept six appropriate sentences containing
   both a subject and an object. **(6 marks)**

3 **a.** There are ten girls skipping. ✓ **(1 mark)**

4 Accept appropriate sentences. Examples:
   a. My mum likes baking **chocolate cakes**.
      (1 mark)
   b. Do you like drawing **cartoon pictures**?
      (1 mark)
   c. My sister is great at riding **horses**
      and ponies. **(1 mark)**
   d. We've all been playing **card and**
      board games. **(1 mark)**

Active and passive voice
pages 32–33

1 Accept two appropriate sentences in the
   active voice, e.g. The children went to
   school on the bus. **(2 marks)**

2 Accept two appropriate sentences in the passive voice, e.g. The boys were taken to the match by their dads. **(2 marks)**

3 **a.** The children were taken by their parents to the disco for the Year 6 treat.
   OR: The children were taken to the disco for the Year 6 treat. **(1 mark)**

   b. Everest was conquered by Sir Edmund Hillary and Sherpa Tenzing in 1953.
   OR: Everest was conquered in 1953 by Sir Edmund Hillary and Sherpa Tenzing. **(1 mark)**

   c. The apple pie was burned by the cooks because the oven was too hot. **(1 mark)**

   d. The rubbish was thrown out by Millie when the bin started to overflow. **(1 mark)**

   e. My big sister's tooth was extracted by the dentist. **(1 mark)**

   f. Finally, the champion's cup was won by the determined junior team.
   OR: The champion's cup was finally won by the determined junior team. **(1 mark)**

4

Sentence	Active voice	Passive voice
The angry wasps stung the children.	✓	
My mother brought my friends and me to the cinema.	✓	
A family was rescued from the blaze by a fireman.		✓
We were given an ultimatum by our teacher.		✓
The thieves were being pursued.		✓
We left our picnic blanket by the edge of the river.	✓	

(6 marks)

5 **a.** An enthusiastic dog-walker walked my energetic dog all week.
   OR: All week, an enthusiastic dog-walker walked my energetic dog. **(1 mark)**

   b. The team completed the transatlantic race in record time. **(1 mark)**

   c. The emergency team received three phone calls last night.
   OR: Last night, the emergency team received three phone calls. **(1 mark)**

   d. The young journalist wrote a fascinating newspaper article. **(1 mark)**

Direct speech
pages 34–35

1 When Benji heard the thunder in the middle of the night, he said it was the loudest noise he'd ever heard. <u>"Make it go away!"</u> he shouted. His mum said that it couldn't hurt him and it might help to count the seconds between the thunder claps and the lightning bolts. <u>"It's nature, sweetheart, and it won't last forever,"</u> she reassured him. <u>"Come, on let's count together."</u> <u>"One, two, three, four…"</u> they counted. By eight, Benji was already asleep. **(3 marks)**

2 **a.** "I would really like to go to the cinema to see that new Spiderman film," Paul said. **(1 mark)**

   b. "We knew that eventually we would move to America," the children told their neighbours. **(1 mark)**

   c. "Start running now!" Jack screamed. **(1 mark)**

   d. Taylor said, "I hope I remembered to put the chocolate brownies in the picnic basket." **(1 mark)**

   e. "Have you brought your library book in today?" asked the librarian. **(1 mark)**

3 **a.** "Will you play football with me, Billy?" asked Max. **(1 mark)**

   b. "Everyone can come to my house for tea!" announced Harry. **(1 mark)**

   c. "Score!" shouted all the Year 6 spectators to the lacrosse team. **(1 mark)**

   d. "Could I have some extra time in the reading test?" Honor asked her teacher. **(1 mark)**

4 Answers will vary. Examples:
   whispered; muttered; sighed; agreed; stuttered; uttered; shouted; roared; screamed; shrieked
   (up to 10 marks)

Informal and formal speech
pages 36–37

1 **a.** Informal speech is a relaxed way of speaking where we might use slang, abbreviations and colloquialisms. In formal speech we use Standard English, applying all the rules of English grammar. **(2 marks)**

   b. We use informal speech when chatting, texting or emailing friends and family.
   We use formal speech when talking or writing to our teachers, other adults beyond our family or when delivering a speech. **(2 marks)**

2 **a.** informal **(1 mark)**
   b. formal **(1 mark)**
   c. informal **(1 mark)**
   d. formal **(1 mark)**
   e. informal **(1 mark)**
   f. informal **(1 mark)**
   g. formal **(1 mark)**

Answers

3 Answers will vary. Appropriate use of informal language, slang and colloquialisms. Examples:

Saturday
Got up dead late, stuffed my breakfast down me and hopped on the 214 bus to town. Met Bryony for a cuppa – hot choc, my fave!

Sunday
Watched the team play footie. They won! YEAH! Got home, grabbed a butty then met Bryony again 'coz she needed help with the well hard homework that the dragon set this week.

(4 marks)

4 a. Her Majesty requires that all visitors **be** respectful of the palace grounds. **(1 mark)**

b. If only we **were** able to join you on holiday! **(1 mark)**

5 Answers will vary. Example:
Good morning everybody. I'd like to extend a warm welcome to author Joseph Welsh. As many of you know from reading his books, Joseph writes adventure stories, often based on his own experiences. As a young child, Joseph… etc. **(4 marks)**

6 a. We aren't going to the park because we have visitors. **(1 mark)**

b. Pick those books up now or else I'll be very cross. **(1 mark)**

c. She would have helped you if you had asked. **(1 mark)**

d. I don't want any chips with my chicken. **(1 mark)**

PUNCTUATION

Capital letters and full stops
pages 38–39

1 We use punctuation marks as 'signposts' to help us understand a text. **(1 mark)**

2 We use capital letters at the start of a sentence and for proper nouns; full stops come at the end of a sentence. **(1 mark)**

3 **W**hen **M**aggie and **J**ack reached the outskirts of **L**ondon they were quite overwhelmed at the sight of some of the iconic buildings. **L**ooming before them were the **H**ouses of **P**arliament, then **B**ig **B**en, next **W**estminster **A**bbey and **S**t **P**aul's

Cathedral. **T**aking a boat on the **R**iver **T**hames, the children were wide-eyed in awe and amazement as they saw the city from a different perspective. **A**ll they could think about was how impressed their teacher, **M**rs **M**uggins, would be when they went in to school on **M**onday morning. **(4 marks)**

4

Sentence	Correct?
My brother said his friend pat was going to watch the new harry potter film with him.	
At breezybank primary school, the best teachers, in my opinion, are mrs mason and mr burns.	
after a long wait in London, the children got on the bus to Cambridge and went home.	
My next adventure will be to take a raft down the River Ganges in India.	✓
Every wednesday, I go to the swimming baths with Claire and Sam.	

(1 mark)

5 a. "I'm off to the shops now," said Bill to his sister. "There's a special discount on at Sweetsavers." **(1 mark)**

b. We couldn't understand how Maddie had forgotten her homework for the second time in a week. Our teacher had told her many times. **(1 mark)**

c. Looking out of the window, Tom was struggling to see his dad's Volvo through the fog. Then it started to clear and before he knew it Tom was outside playing in the sunshine. **(1 mark)**

d. Megan and Amy were off to Paris to visit the Eiffel Tower which they hoped to climb to the top. They were going with their cousin Arthur who speaks French fluently. **(1 mark)**

e. I watched The Lion King when we went to London. It was truly amazing and probably the best performance I've ever seen. I would actually go back and watch it again. **(1 mark)**

Question marks and exclamation marks

pages 40–41

1 We use question marks to show someone has asked a question. **(1 mark)**

2 We use exclamation marks to show someone is exclaiming or sometimes when giving a command. **(1 mark)**

3 a. It really was the most dreadful weather! **(1 mark)**
   b. "I'm going home now, aren't you?" **(1 mark)**
   c. "There's not much point in staying any longer, is there?" **(1 mark)**
   d. "Wow! Look at the flooding further down the river bank! **(1 mark)**
   e. Had they really arrived that morning in glorious sunshine? **(1 mark)**

4 Accept any suitable answers. Examples:
   a. What did the man look like? **(1 mark)**
   b. Who did you see in the park? **(1 mark)**
   c. How did you make that meal? **(1 mark)**
   d. When do you like to read? **(1 mark)**

5 b. Isn't it amazing to think that soon we will see another astronaut land on the Moon? ✓
   e. The pain in my leg is so excruciatingly bad I can hardly breathe! ✓
   (2 marks)

6 a. The weather's gone really cold, <u>hasn't it?</u> **(1 mark)**
   b. We are surely going to beat this team, <u>aren't we?</u> **(1 mark)**
   c. Last time we rode our scooters to the park, you fell off, <u>didn't you?</u> **(1 mark)**
   d. I don't think I've ever told you how grateful I am for your help, <u>have I?</u> **(1 mark)**

Commas

pages 42–43

1 Answers will vary. Examples:
   To separate items in a list; to indicate a brief pause in a sentence to make the meaning clearer and avoid ambiguity; before or after direct speech; to separate a clause from the rest of the sentence; to separate a fronted adverbial from the rest of the sentence.
   (4 marks)

2 a. Alfie consulted the recipe book and noted he would need sultanas, sugar, eggs, plain flour and cherries. **(1 mark)**
   b. The animals at the zoo ranged from fierce-looking tigers, hissing snakes and cheeky chimps to elegant giraffes, squawking cockatoos and lazy lions. **(1 mark)**

c. With only minutes to spare before the flight, we threw our thermal vests, ski socks, fur-lined gloves and scarves into our cases, bags and rucksacks. **(1 mark)**

3 a. "Let's eat, Erin!" exclaimed a very hungry Milo. **(1 mark)**
   b. My friend's hobbies are cooking, her family and her pets. **(1 mark)**
   c. The pupil, thinks the teacher, is improving in Maths. **(1 mark)**
   d. The boy walked on, his head throbbing in pain. **(1 mark)**
   e. "That's a foul, striker!" shouted the referee. **(1 mark)**

4 a. "We really do need to get our skates on," said Mum. **(1 mark)**
   b. I looked at her in surprise and replied, "But surely we have two hours before it starts?" **(1 mark)**
   c. Mum raised her eyebrows, saying, "The traffic will be horrendous at this time of night." **(1 mark)**
   d. "Well, why don't we get the train? We could relax then and read our books," I suggested. **(1 mark)**
   e. "There's one at 7:08 from our local station," Mum said. **(1 mark)**

5 Answers will vary. Examples:
   a. We all trooped outside, **although it was raining heavily,** and played until our parents shouted at us to come inside. **(1 mark)**
   b. My collection of stamps, **which I kept in a leather-bound album,** sold on the Internet for an amazing sum of money. **(1 mark)**
   c. The neighbours to our right, **whose garden has always been a mess,** finally mowed their lawn and weeded their flower beds. **(1 mark)**
   d. My uncle Ted, **despite being in his eighties,** still managed to run the London Marathon. **(1 mark)**

Inverted commas

pages 44–45

1 a. In direct speech, to indicate the start and end of someone speaking. **(1 mark)**
   b. For quotations. **(1 mark)**
   c. For nicknames and other titles. **(1 mark)**

2 a. "I've just discovered that our cousins are coming for the weekend," said Brogan. **(1 mark)**
   b. Joe was delighted and said, "We should take them to the forest and go exploring!" **(1 mark)**
   c. "Yes, let's build a den too!" exclaimed Brogan excitedly. "We'll have to take a picnic." **(1 mark)**

d. "I'm not sure Sarah will come," said Joe. "Not after last time." **(1 mark)**

e. "The incident with the spider wasn't my fault," responded Brogan defensively. **(1 mark)**

3 b. "I've just eaten two cakes and a packet of crisps", Rita told Dev. ☑

d. "We have to go now"! Dad said firmly, "Otherwise we will be late." ☑ **(2 marks)**

4 a. The boy they call "Mad Max" has just been seen hurtling towards the park.
Reason: <u>Nickname</u> **(2 marks)**

b. I've just finished reading "Harry Potter and the Philosopher's Stone".
Reason: <u>Book title</u> **(2 marks)**

c. Last night we watched "The Simpsons" on television.
Reason: <u>Title of programme</u> **(2 marks)**

d. The song I loved best at the concert was "One Way or Another".
Reason: <u>Song title</u> **(2 marks)**

e. I've just read an article about the Queen. One comment says: "Her Majesty is always in bed by ten." Another says: "Her Majesty likes cereal and toast for breakfast."
Reason: <u>Quotations</u> **(2 marks)**

Apostrophes
pages 46–47

1 She's always late for school. **(1 mark)**

2 My mum's birthday is today. **(1 mark)**

3

Word in full	Contraction	Word in full	Contraction
We have	**We've**	There are	**There're**
There is	**There's**	I would	**I'd**
She is	**She's**	I am	**I'm**
will not	**won't**	was not	**wasn't**
would have	**would've**	should not	**shouldn't**
is not	**isn't**	shall not	**shan't**

(6 marks)

4 b. We'll probably go to the caravan where there's always so much to do. ☑ **(1 mark)**

5 a. Mrs Smith's umbrella. **(1 mark)**

b. Sinead's homework was ruined by the rain. **(1 mark)**

c. The sun's rays beat down on the arid desert sand. **(1 mark)**

d. That dog's barks could be heard for miles and miles. **(1 mark)**

e. The girls' books need to go back to the library today. **(1 mark)**

f. Our class's furniture is going to be replaced. **(1 mark)**

6 a. It's almost dark so its best we head home before it's too late to catch the bus. **(3 marks)**
☑   ☒   ☑

b. Its been drizzling on and off all day so it's time the weather made it's mind up. **(3 marks)**
☒   ☑   ☒

Punctuation to indicate parenthesis
pages 48–49

1 a. The children's books (all of which are a bit tatty and worn) have finally been returned to the school library. **(1 mark)**

b. My brother Miles (the one who's mad about music) is going to a concert tonight. **(1 mark)**

c. How could anyone (even the most hard-hearted) not look at that newborn puppy and smile? **(1 mark)**

d. I've said before (and no doubt I will say it many times again) that I don't like being teased by my big sister. **(1 mark)**

e. Look in the far corner of the park (the spot where there's a fountain) and you will see the lads playing football. **(1 mark)**

f. I'm very good at reading (and writing for that matter) but I don't perform well in tests. **(1 mark)**

2 Answers will vary. Examples:

a. After some time we went home – **battered and bruised** – and had hot baths and bowls of soup. **(1 mark)**

b. With only minutes to spare – **two to be exact** – we managed to get the last train. **(1 mark)**

c. Imagine my delight when chicken and carrots – **my favourite** – were served on the plane. **(1 mark)**

d. The winning goal – **scored by Rooney** – was the best of the match. **(1 mark)**

e. My best friend's dad – **Mr Weasley** – took us to school this morning. **(1 mark)**

f. We went to the local cinema – **the Odeon** – to watch the new Disney film. **(1 mark)**

3 d. My brother, short but very strong, stopped the thieves from getting away. ☑ **(1 mark)**

Colons, semi-colons, dashes and bullet points
pages 50–51

1 a. You will need the following: scissors, glue, paper, paint and water. **(1 mark)**

b. I have only one dream: to play for a premier league team. **(1 mark)**

c. The Head Teacher made her last announcement of the evening: there would be tea and coffee served in the staffroom. **(1 mark)**

d. Narrator: Tonight, thankfully, was not to be Bird Pie Night! **(1 mark)**

2 a. I've always loved the idea of living by the sea; in time, I'm sure, we'll make the move. **(1 mark)**

b. There were children from all over the world on the residential trip: Helga from Frankfurt in Germany; Berndt from Zurich in Switzerland; Manuel from Lisbon in Portugal and Rory from Belfast in Northern Ireland. **(2 marks)**

3 a. Finally we were at the top of the highest mountain in the world – now for the descent. **(1 mark)**

b. I had reached the end of my magical journey – or was it *really* the end? **(1 mark)**

c. The Maths paper was very hard – so hard that I think I've failed. **(1 mark)**

d. I turned a corner and surveyed the scene – a horror that words could not describe. **(1 mark)**

4 Answers will vary. Examples:

a. To make beans on toast you will need the following ingredients:
- beans
- bread
- butter **(1 mark)**

b. Before going on holiday, the children packed the following:
- towels
- swimwear
- shorts **(1 mark)**

c. My top four favourite celebrities are the following:
- Harry Stiles
- Taylor Swift
- Daniel Radcliffe
- David Beckham **(1 mark)**

Hyphens and ellipses
pages 52–53

1

A	B	C
kind	minded	kind-hearted
well	tempered	well-known
fair	living	fair-minded
dark	coloured	dark-haired
long	known	long-living
multi	hearted	multi-coloured
bad	haired	bad-tempered

(7 marks)

2 a. pre-view **(1 mark)**

b. re-form **(1 mark)**

c. re-present **(1 mark)**

d. re-cover **(1 mark)**

3 a. Rebecca stared out of the window and considered her options. She could stay … or she could go … **(1 mark)**

b. As Joe approached the cave, he heard a groaning noise … or maybe it was a growl … **(1 mark)**

c. Standing on top of the cliff, Jake held his breath and looked down at the sea below. One … two … three. He jumped. **(1 mark)**

4 Ellipsis is used to show that there is text between the last word before the ellipsis and the first word after the ellipsis. **(1 mark)**

VOCABULARY AND SPELLING

Synonyms and antonyms
pages 54–55
Synonyms

1 A synonym is a word with the same or similar meaning as another word. **(1 mark)**

2 Answers may vary. Examples:

Adjectives	Synonyms	Nouns	Synonyms
noisy	**loud**	present	**gift**
angry	**cross**	bravery	**courage**
delicious	**tasty**	drink	**beverage**
scary	**frightening**	argument	**quarrel**
untidy	**messy**	drawing	**sketch**
easy	**straightforward**	walk	**stroll**

(12 marks)

3 Answers may vary. Examples:

a. exclaimed **(1 mark)**

b. strolled **(1 mark)**

c. sketched **(1 mark)**

d. baked **(1 mark)**

e. disrupted **(1 mark)**

f. irritates **(1 mark)**

Antonyms

1 An antonym is a word opposite in meaning to another word. **(1 mark)**

2 **c.** My dog's bed consists of a large cushion and **firm** sides. ☑ **(1 mark)**

3 Answers may vary. Examples:
   a. cold; heavy **(1 mark)**
   b. bright; powerful **(1 mark)**
   c. raised; over **(1 mark)**

Prefixes
pages 56–57

1 A prefix is a string of letters added to the start of a word to turn it into another word. **(1 mark)**

2

Prefix	Word	New word
il	accessible	**illogical**
ir	ability	**irrespective**
dis	apprehension	**disability**
mis	logical	**misapprehension**
im	respective	**implausible**
in	plausible	**inaccessible**

(6 marks)

3 **a.** disrespect **(1 mark)**
   b. misrepresent **(1 mark)**
   c. disagree **(1 mark)**
   d. misunderstanding **(1 mark)**
   e. misinterpreted **(1 mark)**

4 Not functioning correctly. **(1 mark)**

5 **b.** The teacher said my artwork was incomplete. ☑ **(1 mark)**
   d. It is quite improbable that the stadium will be finished by next year. ☑ **(1 mark)**

Prefixes from Latin and Greek

1 **a.** two **(1 mark)**
   b. big / above **(1 mark)**
   c. distant / far **(1 mark)**
   d. half **(1 mark)**

2 Answers may vary. Examples:

auto		aqua	pre
autobiography	autograph	aquaplane	preschool
autocratic/ autocracy	automatic	aquamarine	premeditated
automobile	autopilot	aquarium	predate

(12 marks)

Suffixes
pages 58–59

1 A suffix is a letter string added to the end of a root word, changing or adding to its meaning. **(1 mark)**

2

	Adjective	Adverb
depend	**dependable**	**dependably**
comfort	**comfortable**	**comfortably**
rely	**reliable**	**reliably**
notice	**noticeable**	**noticeably**

(4 marks)

3

	Adjective	Adverb
horror	**horrible**	**horribly**
terror	**terrible**	**terribly**
sense	**sensible**	**sensibly**
reverse	**reversible**	**reversibly**
audio	**audible**	**audibly**

(5 marks)

4 **a.** vicious **(1 mark)**
   b. malicious **(1 mark)**
   c. spacious **(1 mark)**
   d. gracious **(1 mark)**

5 **a.** ambitious **(1 mark)**
   b. infectious **(1 mark)**
   c. nutritious **(1 mark)**
   d. fictitious **(1 mark)**

Suffixes
pages 60–61

1 **a.** residential **(1 mark)**
   b. financial **(1 mark)**
   c. influential **(1 mark)**
   d. facial **(1 mark)**

2 **a.** innocence **(1 mark)**
   b. defence **(1 mark)**
   c. dominance **(1 mark)**
   d. tolerance **(1 mark)**
   e. hesitance **(1 mark)**
   f. obedience **(1 mark)**

3 **a.** Walking in the Peak District was a real **endurance** test. **(1 mark)**
   b. The Head Teacher thanked us for our **compliance** with the school uniform rule. **(1 mark)**
   c. My **reliance** on my brother to help me with my homework has got to stop! **(1 mark)**

Answers

d. The instructions said that after the **appliance** of glue, the two sides would stick together. **(1 mark)**

e. After much **reassurance** from my friends, I felt able to confront the bully. **(1 mark)**

f. The **disappearance** of our dog in the middle of the night was a complete mystery. **(1 mark)**

4 **a.** interference **(1 mark)**
   b. perseverance **(1 mark)**
   c. adherence **(1 mark)**

Suffixes from Greek

1 Answers will vary. Examples:

Suffix	Word	Meaning
phone	xylophone	A percussion instrument
meter	pedometer	A device which measures how far you run, walk or cycle
logy	geology	The study of rocks
phobia	agoraphobia	A fear of public places

(8 marks)

Tricky spellings

pages 62–63

The rule 'i before e except after c but only when it rhymes with bee'

1 Answers will vary. Examples:
   field; piece; shield; ceiling; deceive; conceive

(6 marks)

2 **a.** receipt **(1 mark)**
   b. deceive **(1 mark)**
   c. perceived **(1 mark)**
   d. ceiling **(1 mark)**
   e. conceived **(1 mark)**
   f. received **(1 mark)**

3 **a.** eight **(1 mark)**
   b. weight **(1 mark)**
   c. beige **(1 mark)**
   d. weird **(1 mark)**
   e. protein **(1 mark)**
   f. caffeine **(1 mark)**

Words ending in fer

1

Word	Add suffixes	Is the **fer** stressed?
refer	referral	✓
	reference	✗
	referred	✓
transfer	transferal	✓
	transference	✗
	transferred	✓
prefer	preference	✗
	preferred	✓
infer	inference	✗
	inferred	✓

(10 marks)

Tricky spellings

pages 64–65

Letter string ough

1 Answers will vary. Examples:

oh sound	aw sound	uff sound	ow sound	o sound
although	brought	rough	plough	trough
dough	thought	tough	drought	

(1 mark per word)

2 **a.** My brother **brought** me some **cough** medicine because he **thought** it would make me better. **(1 mark)**

   b. The **rough** seas were bad **enough** but once on land, a **bough** from a **tough** old oak tree snapped and landed on my head. **(1 mark)**

Silent letters

1 A silent letter is a letter that we don't pronounce. **(1 mark)**

2 **a.** assig̲n **b.** de̲bt **c.** crum̲b
   d. nes̲tle **e.** condem̲n **f.** h̲onest
   g. foreig̲n **h.** s̲word **i.** k̲nowledge
   j. hym̲n **k.** sc̲issors **l.** recei̲pt

(12 marks)

3 **a.** Wednesday   handkerchief **(1 mark)**
   b. jostling   silhouette **(1 mark)**
   c. receipt   succumbing **(1 mark)**
   d. solemn   echoed **(1 mark)**

The prefix psych

1 **a.** psychology **(1 mark)**
   b. psychiatrist **(1 mark)**
   c. psychic **(1 mark)**
   d. psychedelic **(1 mark)**

The letters ph

1 Answers will vary. Examples:
pharaoh, pharmacy, photo, phrase, physical, physics
alphabet, apostrophe, graph, geography, sphere, trophy **(12 marks)**

Tricky plurals
pages 66–67
Words ending in o

1

Singular	Plural
piano	**pianos**
hero	**heroes**
mango	**mangos / mangoes**
studio	**studios**
banjo	**banjos**
echo	**echoes**
kilo	**kilos**
potato	**potatoes**
torpedo	**torpedoes**

(9 marks)

Words ending in f, ff and fe

1 a. shelves **(1 mark)**
   b. knives **(1 mark)**
   c. lives **(1 mark)**
   d. wolves **(1 mark)**
   e. thieves **(1 mark)**

2 a. The tribal <u>chiefs</u> agreed to respect each others' different <u>beliefs</u>. **(1 mark)**
   b. From the top of the <u>roofs</u> came billowing <u>puffs</u> of white smoke. **(1 mark)**
   c. The pirate's <u>bluffs</u> had gone on long enough so the captain dropped anchor in front of the towering white <u>cliffs</u> and confronted him. **(1 mark)**
   d. The garden party <u>chefs</u> put on <u>waterproofs</u> when it started to rain. **(1 mark)**
   e. The little <u>waifs</u> were poorly dressed and underfed after being looked after by two beastly <u>oafs</u>. **(1 mark)**

Words with two possible plurals

1

Singular	Plural 1	Plural 2
scarf	**scarves**	**scarfs**
wharf	**wharves**	**wharfs**
dwarf	**dwarves**	**dwarfs**
hoof	**hooves**	**hoofs**

(4 marks)

Homophones and homonyms
pages 68–69
Homophones

1 A homophone is a word that sounds the same as another word but has a different spelling and different meaning. **(1 mark)**

2 d. I looked **through** the window and saw a huge **bear** ambling about in the garden. ✓ **(1 mark)**

3

Word	Homophone(s)	Word	Homophone(
pause	**paws**	whether	**weather**
piece	**peace**	find	**fined**
pour	**pore / poor**	great	**grate**
knew	**new / gnu**	shore	**sure**
buy	**bye / by**	night	**knight**
morning	**mourning**	sent	**scent / cent**
profit	**prophet**	root	**route**

(14 marks)

Near homophones

1 Near homophones don't sound exactly the same but are similar enough for people often to misspell them. **(1 mark)**

2 a. The hot, sunny weather had a therapeutic (effect) on the whole family. **(1 mark)**
   b. The teacher gave the parents some great (advice) about the tests. **(1 mark)**
   c. The fireman couldn't gain (access) to the burning building. **(1 mark)**
   d. Last night the swimming pool was full of screaming (adolescents) **(1 mark)**
   e. I bought the latest (edition) of my favourite magazine. **(1 mark)**
   f. We all found it difficult to (accept) that our cat had gone. **(1 mark)**

Homonyms

1 Homonyms sound the same AND have the same spelling as another word but have a different meaning. It is usually obvious from the context which meaning is intended. **(1 mark)**

2 Answers will vary. Examples:
   a i. I watch my brother play tennis.
      ii. I got a new watch for my birthday. **(2 marks)**
   b i. The dog's bark sounded angry.
      ii. We collected tree bark for our project. **(2 marks)**

c i. Dad takes the train to work.
  ii. Mum likes to train every morning before work.
                                            (2 marks)

d i. My older sister is fair, whereas I am dark.
  ii. It's not fair that my older sister gets more pocket money than me. **(2 marks)**

MIXED PRACTICE QUESTIONS

pages 70–78

1 <u>despite</u> **(1 mark)**

2 fell ✓ **(1 mark)**

3 irresponsible ✓ **(1 mark)**

4 The thieves were arrested as they tried to leave town. ✓ **(1 mark)**

5 <u>Cautiously</u>, the boys crept into the cave, treading <u>carefully</u> as they went. **(1 mark)**

6 When **I/we/she/he/they** arrived at our mother's bedside, **I/we/she/he/they** could see that **she** had greatly improved. **(1 mark)**

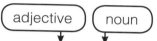

7 Phil studied the detailed map then put it back neatly in his waterproof rucksack. **(1 mark)**

adjective ↑   noun ↑

8 What a fuss about nothing! ✓ **(1 mark)**

9 Answers will vary. Examples: **(1 mark)**
exhausted; wiped out; wrecked

10 Our football team finally won (<u>after</u> / since) many defeats, (therefore / <u>however</u>) we know we have a long way to go before we can claim the league cup. **(1 mark)**

11 Ushma's dog teases my cats. ✓
They were swimming in the sea early this morning. ✓ **(1 mark)**

12 I always loved the end of term when <u>we'd</u> finished our exams and the days were long. **(1 mark)**

13 My younger brother loves peas (yet) hates carrots. **(1 mark)**

14 a. My cousin (the one from America) is always talking about celebrities. **(1 mark)**
b. When I get home in the evening (no matter how late) I like to relax with a book. **(1 mark)**
c. The summer holiday months (July and August) are a great time to visit the Lake District. **(1 mark)**
d. The Head Teacher laughed happily (not a common sight I can tell you) during the Year 6 production. **(1 mark)**

15 The family we met on holiday, all of whom were very pleasant, contacted us last week. **(1 mark)**

16 a. We <u>love</u> to visit the seaside but last year it was a bit of a washout. **(1 mark)**
b. My dog liked our long walks when he was young but lately he <u>becomes</u> very tired. **(1 mark)**
c. All through the school year, we worked hard but now <u>is</u> the time to relax. **(1 mark)**

17 My brother went to school today, <u>despite having his arm in plaster</u>. **(1 mark)**

18 "So you think you're going to win the match tomorrow, <u>do you</u>?" **(1 mark)**

19 "Hurry up or you'll be late for school!" shouted my mum. "It's almost 9 o'clock."
"Why don't we take the short cut through the field?" I asked. "We'd be there in no time." **(1 mark)**

20 a. Abby's cat has gone missing but he's wearing his blue collar so he'll be easily spotted. **(1 mark)**
b. Mum's been waiting ages for Katie's bus but it's clearly late. **(1 mark)**
c. We're so thrilled that Jake's passed his exams that we think it'd be good to celebrate. **(1 mark)**

21

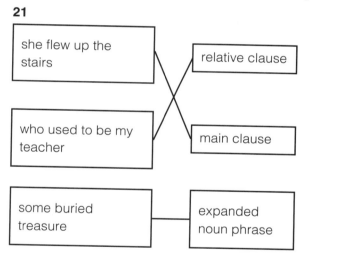

                                      (1 mark)

22 Stella's reading is more advanced than Chloe's. ✓ **(1 mark)**

23 When I pack for a weekend away in the countryside, I take lots of warm clothes: sweaters, boots, gloves and a coat. **(1 mark)**

24 After having <u>eaten</u> our breakfast, we jumped into the car and headed off. **(1 mark)**

25 were ✓ **(1 mark)**

26 I will finish my homework project this evening. ✓ **(1 mark)**

27 You need to water the flowers **and** the plants, **even though** it rained in the night. Here is a watering can **but** you might prefer to use a jug **or** a hose. **(1 mark)**

28 You need to get a move on or you'll be late, **won't you?** **(1 mark)**

29 *Shall we start to eat, Mum?* The speaker is asking their mum if they should start to eat. *Shall we start to eat, Mum?* The speaker is asking someone else if they should start to eat their mum. **(1 mark)**

30 After an extremely long flight, I was relieved to get into my comfortable bed for a sleep. **(1 mark)**

31 To make your cheese sandwich, you will need the following:
- bread
- cheese
- butter **(1 mark)**

(Ingredients can be capitalised and commas or semi-colons at end of first two bullet points acceptable if full stop after 'butter'.)

32 There isn't time for us to eat because **it's** already 9 o'clock. **(1 mark)**

33 Mrs Courtney's antique vase suddenly tipped over. **(1 mark)**

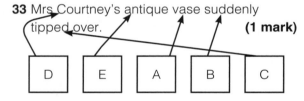

| D | E | A | B | C |

34 After a long day in the park, the exhausted children **were** glad to get home.
OR: ... the exhausted **child** was glad to get home. **(1 mark)**

35

Sentence	Apostrophe used in a contraction	Apostrophe used to show possession
I daren't tell the teacher I forgot my homework.	✓	
Rebecca's pony likes apples.		✓
The children's books are in the library.		✓
We've been told to stand outside the office.	✓	

(4 marks)

36 illegal **(1 mark)**

37 A volcano is a mountain that (<u>opens</u> / is opening) downward to molten rock lying below the surface of the Earth. With the build-up of pressure, eruptions (occurred / <u>occur</u>). Gases and rock (shoots / <u>shoot</u>) up through the opening, filling the air with fragments of lava. **(3 marks)**

38 accident ✓ **(1 mark)**

39 <u>Turn</u> to the next page and <u>read</u> the first two paragraphs. What do you think made Theo react that way? **(1 mark)**

40 Mrs Rothwell's computer screen needed to be fixed. **(1 mark)**

5 Tick **two** boxes to indicate the sentences which are correctly punctuated. **(2 marks)**

a. I really thought you, of all people, would have behaved more sensibly? ☐

b. Isn't it amazing to think that soon we will see another astronaut land on the Moon? ☐

c. Go away – you deliberately pushed me over when I was trying to score? ☐

d. I'm so excited about our trip to New York next week, aren't you! ☐

e. The pain in my leg is so excruciatingly bad I can hardly breathe! ☐

6 Add suitable **question tags** to the following sentences, finishing with the correct **punctuation**.
An example has been done for you.

You have tidied your bedroom, *haven't you?*...............

a. The weather's gone really cold, ... **(1 mark)**

b. We are surely going to beat this team, ... **(1 mark)**

c. Last time we rode our scooters to the park, you fell off, ... **(1 mark)**

d. I don't think I've ever told you how grateful I am for
your help, ... **(1 mark)**

Top tip! You might see small **i** for **I** used in a text message but you should only ever write it with a capital **I**!

Total $\frac{}{18}$

1 Write four places where you might use **commas**.

a. .... **(1 mark)**

b. .... **(1 mark)**

c. .... **(1 mark)**

d. .... **(1 mark)**

2 Insert the missing **commas** in these sentences.

a. Alfie consulted the recipe book and noted he would need sultanas sugar eggs plain flour and cherries. **(1 mark)**

b. The animals at the zoo ranged from fierce-looking tigers hissing snakes and cheeky chimps to elegant giraffes squawking cockatoos and lazy lions. **(1 mark)**

c. With only minutes to spare before the flight, we threw our thermal vests ski socks fur-lined gloves and scarves into our cases bags and rucksacks. **(1 mark)**

3 Position **commas** in the following sentences to avoid ambiguity.

a. "Let's eat Erin!" exclaimed a very hungry Milo. **(1 mark)**

b. My friend's hobbies are cooking her family and her pets. **(1 mark)**

c. The pupil thinks the teacher is improving in Maths. **(1 mark)**

d. The boy walked on his head throbbing in pain. **(1 mark)**

e. "That's a foul striker!" shouted the referee. **(1 mark)**

4 Insert **commas** in the correct places in the following direct speech.

a. "We really do need to get our skates on " said Mum. **(1 mark)**

b. I looked at her in surprise and replied "But surely we have two hours before it starts?" **(1 mark)**

c. Mum raised her eyebrows, saying "The traffic will be horrendous at this time of night." **(1 mark)**

d. "Well, why don't we get the train? We could relax then and read our books " I suggested. **(1 mark)**

e. "There's one at 7:08 from our local station " Mum said. **(1 mark)**

5 Complete each sentence by writing a subordinate clause in the gap. Use the words in brackets. Add commas where you think they are needed. An example has been done for you.

The stooped, white-haired man, *who ran from the crime scene*, was asked to help the police with their investigation.

a. We all trooped outside (although) ....
and played until our parents shouted at us to come inside. **(1 mark)**

b. My collection of stamps (which) ....
sold on the Internet for an amazing sum of money. **(1 mark)**

c. The neighbours to our right (whose) ....
finally mowed their lawn and weeded their flower beds. **(1 mark)**

d. My uncle Ted (despite) .... still managed
to run the London Marathon. **(1 mark)**

Remember commas are punctuation signposts to help you know when to take a breath or pause.

Total $\frac{}{21}$

1 Write three places where we use **inverted commas**.

a. .... **(1 mark)**

b. .... **(1 mark)**

c. .... **(1 mark)**

2 Insert inverted commas and any other missing punctuation in the following direct speech.

a. I've just discovered that our cousins are coming for the weekend said Brogan. **(1 mark)**

b. Joe was delighted and said We should take them to the forest and go exploring! **(1 mark)**

c. Yes, let's build a den too exclaimed Brogan excitedly. We'll have to take a picnic. **(1 mark)**

d. I'm not sure Sarah will come said Joe Not after last time. **(1 mark)**

e. The incident with the spider wasn't my fault responded Brogan defensively. **(1 mark)**

3 Which **two** sentences are **not** correctly punctuated?
Tick **two**. **(2 marks)**

a. "How many environmental issues are on today's agenda?" asked the Year 6 House Captain. ☐

b. "I've just eaten two cakes and a packet of crisps", Rita told Dev. ☐

c. "I've not seen the cartoon you are talking about," Phil said. ☐

d. "We have to go now"! Dad said firmly, "Otherwise we will be late." ☐

e. "I've just seen our friends walking down the road with their new dog!" ☐

4 The following sentences need inverted commas for different reasons. Rewrite them, inserting the inverted commas and say why they are needed.

a. The boy they call Mad Max has just been seen hurtling towards the park. **(2 marks)**

....

Reason: ....

b. I've just finished reading Harry Potter and the Philosopher's Stone. **(2 marks)**

....

Reason: ....

c. Last night we watched The Simpsons on television. **(2 marks)**

....

Reason: ....

d. The song I loved best at the concert was One Way or Another. **(2 marks)**

....

Reason: ....

e. I've just read an article about the Queen. One comment says: Her Majesty is always in bed by ten. Another says: Her Majesty likes cereal and toast for breakfast. **(2 marks)**

....

....

Reason: ....

> *I'd like to watch "The Simpsons" tonight if I get my homework finished.*

Total $\frac{}{20}$

1 Insert the missing **apostrophe** to show a **contraction** in the sentence below. **(1 mark)**

Shes always late for school.

2 Insert the missing **apostrophe** to show **possession** in the sentence below. **(1 mark)**

My mums birthday is today.

3 Use an **apostrophe** to turn the following words into **contractions**. **(6 marks)**

Word in full	Contraction	Word in full	Contraction
We have	....	They are	....
There is	....	I would	....
She is	....	I am	....
will not	....	was not	....
would have	....	should not	....
is not	....	shall not	....

4 Which sentence uses **apostrophes for contractions** correctly? **(1 mark)**

Tick the correct one.

a. Iv'e not had my holiday yet because my dads' been too busy at work. ☐

b. We'll probably go to the caravan where there's always so much to do. ☐

c. My cousins' coming to join us for two days which'll be fun. ☐

d. Ther'es not much else Iw'd rather do. ☐

5 Rewrite these sentences so that they contain **apostrophes to show possession**. The first one has been done for you.

The dog belonging to my best friend is really naughty.

My best friend's dog is really naughty. ....

a. The umbrella that belongs to Mrs Smith. **(1 mark)**

....

b. The homework belonging to Sinead was ruined by the rain. **(1 mark)**

....

c. The rays of the sun beat down on the arid desert sand. **(1 mark)**

....

d. The barks of that dog could be heard for miles and miles. **(1 mark)**

....

e. The books belonging to the girls need to go back to the library today. **(1 mark)**

....

f. The furniture belonging to our class is going to be replaced. **(1 mark)**

....

6 Decide whether the following have used **its** or **it's** correctly. Put a tick ✓ or cross ✗ in the boxes.

a. It's almost dark so its best we head home before it's too late to catch the bus.

[ ] [ ] [ ]

(3 marks)

b. Its been drizzling on and off all day so it's time the weather made it's mind up.

[ ] [ ] [ ]

(3 marks)

Remember that **it's** always means **it is** – it is never used to show possession! "The dog wagged **its** tail."

Top tip!

Total ⎯⎯ 21

1 Insert brackets to show **parenthesis** in each sentence.

a. The children's books all of which are a bit tatty and worn have finally been returned to the school library.　**(1 mark)**

b. My brother Miles the one who's mad about music is going to a concert tonight.　**(1 mark)**

c. How could anyone even the most hard-hearted not look at that newborn puppy and smile?　**(1 mark)**

d. I've said before and no doubt I will say it many times again that I don't like being teased by my big sister.　**(1 mark)**

e. Look in the far corner of the park the spot where there's a fountain and you will see the lads playing football.　**(1 mark)**

f. I'm very good at reading and writing for that matter but I don't perform well in tests.　**(1 mark)**

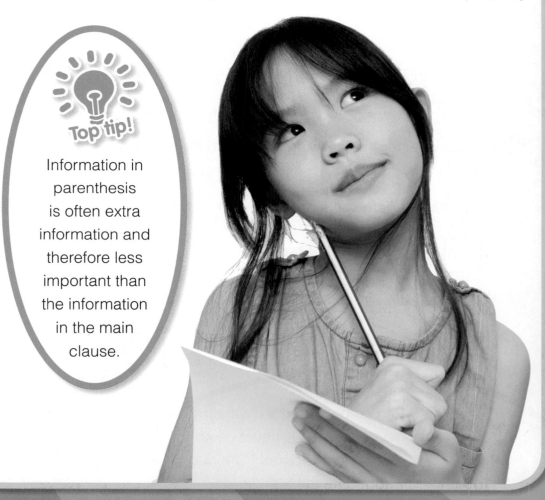

Top tip!

Information in parenthesis is often extra information and therefore less important than the information in the main clause.

2 Write a word, phrase or clause in each gap, using **dashes** around the parenthesis.

a. After some time we went home ....
and had hot baths and bowls of soup. **(1 mark)**

b. With only minutes to spare ....
we managed to get the last train. **(1 mark)**

c. Imagine my delight when chicken and carrots ....
were served on the plane. **(1 mark)**

d. The winning goal ....
was the best of the match. **(1 mark)**

e. My best friend's dad ....
took us to school this morning. **(1 mark)**

f. We went to the local cinema ....
to watch the new Disney film. **(1 mark)**

3 Which sentence uses commas correctly to show parenthesis? **(1 mark)**

Tick the correct sentence.

a. There was a lot, of fuss unnecessarily, after the ice-cream turned out to be the wrong flavour. ☐

b. Ruby not usually, a competitive girl, was first to fling herself over the finish line. ☐

c. When we reached the summit exhausted but exhilarated, we all cheered. ☐

d. My brother, short but very strong, stopped the thieves from getting away. ☐

> **Top tip!** The words in parenthesis are often relative clauses with the relative pronouns omitted. For example:
> My dinner, ready since 6 o'clock, was starting to turn cold.
> My dinner, which had been ready since 6 o'clock, was starting to turn cold.

Total —— 13

1 Insert **colons** in the correct places in the following.

a. You will need the following scissors, glue, paper, paint and water. **(1 mark)**

b. I have only one dream to play for a premier league team. **(1 mark)**

c. The Head Teacher made her last announcement of the evening there would be tea and coffee served in the staffroom. **(1 mark)**

d. Narrator Tonight, thankfully, was not to be Bird Pie Night! **(1 mark)**

2 Insert **semi-colons** in the following sentences.

a. I've always loved the idea of living by the sea in time, I'm sure, we'll make the move. **(1 mark)**

b. There were children from all over the world on the residential trip: Helga from Frankfurt in Germany Berndt from Zurich in Switzerland Manuel from Lisbon in Portugal and Rory from Belfast in Northern Ireland. **(2 marks)**

3 Rewrite the following sentences so that they contain a **single dash**.

a. Finally we were at the top of the highest mountain in the world now for the descent. **(1 mark)**

....

b. I had reached the end of my magical journey or was it *really* the end? **(1 mark)**

....

c. The Maths paper was very hard so hard that I think I've failed. **(1 mark)**

....

d. I turned a corner and surveyed the scene a horror that words could not describe. **(1 mark)**

....

4 Write suitable **bullet points** to follow on from these introductions.

a. To make beans on toast you will need the following ingredients: **(1 mark)**

....

....

....

b. Before going on holiday, the children packed the following: **(1 mark)**

....

....

....

c. My top four favourite celebrities are the following: **(1 mark)**

....

....

....

....

Top tip!

The text following the bullet points does not need to start with a capital letter or end with a full stop. However, if you **do** start with a capital letter, then end with a full stop!

Total $\frac{}{14}$

1 Match each word in column A to a word in column B to make compound words linked by a **hyphen**. Write these in column C. **(7 marks)**

A	B	C
kind	minded	....
well	tempered	....
fair	living	....
dark	coloured	....
long	known	....
multi	hearted	....
bad	haired	....

2 Change the meaning of these words by inserting a **hyphen** between the **prefix** and the root word.

An example has been done for you.

recollect   *re-collect*

a. preview   ....   **(1 mark)**

b. reform   ....   **(1 mark)**

c. represent   ....   **(1 mark)**

d. recover ....   **(1 mark)**

3 Rewrite the following, inserting **two ellipses** in each.

a. Rebecca stared out of the window and considered her options. She could stay or she could go.

(1 mark)

....

....

b. As Joe approached the cave, he heard a groaning noise or maybe it was a growl.

(1 mark)

....

....

c. Standing on top of the cliff, Jake held his breath and looked down at the sea below. One two three. He jumped.

(1 mark)

....

....

4 Explain why **ellipsis** is used in this sentence.

Read the following passage on page 5: "Slowly then... arms."

....

....

.... **(1 mark)**

Top tip!

Remember to hyphenate words at the end of a line at syllable breaks and never send one letter to the next line on its own!

Total $\frac{}{15}$

Synonyms

1 What is a **synonym**? (1 mark)

....

2 Find **synonyms** for the following adjectives and nouns. (12 marks)

Adjectives	Synonyms	Nouns	Synonyms
noisy	....	present	....
angry	....	bravery	....
delicious	....	drink	....
scary	....	argument	....
untidy	....	drawing	....
easy	....	walk	....

3 Choose a **synonym** to replace the verbs in bold.

a. "Let's go for a swim now!" **said** Marcus. (1 mark)

....

b. We **walked** to the village square to see the band. (1 mark)

....

c. The children **did** self-portraits in Art. (1 mark)

....

d. Mum **made** a cake this afternoon. (1 mark)

....

e. The naughty boy **disturbed** the whole class. (1 mark)

....

f. My sister **annoys** me every day. (1 mark)

....

Antonyms

1 What is an **antonym**? **(1 mark)**

....

2 Which sentence uses an antonym for the adjective **soft**? **(1 mark)**

Tick the correct sentence.

a. On Sunday mornings, I wrap myself in my fluffy, feathery duvet. ☐

b. The ball smashed through the window, leaving pointy shards of glass. ☐

c. My dog's bed consists of a large cushion and firm sides. ☐

d. The country road was long, muddy and bumpy. ☐

3 Write **antonyms** for the words in bold.

a. Yesterday was so **hot** that we wore **light** layers on our walk. **(1 mark)**

....

....

b. The lighting in here is very **dull** because the bulbs are so **weak**. **(1 mark)**

....

....

c. We **lowered** the injured dog until we could get him **under** the fence. **(1 mark)**

....

....

Total $\frac{}{24}$

1 Explain what a **prefix** is. **(1 mark)**

....

2 Match each **prefix** with a word to make a new word that is opposite in meaning. **(6 marks)**

Prefix	Word	New word
il	accessible	....
ir	ability	....
dis	apprehension	....
mis	logical	....
im	respective	....
in	plausible	....

3 Rewrite the words in brackets to give them a negative meaning by adding the prefixes **dis** or **mis**.

a. He showed (respect) .... by calling out
while the teacher was speaking. **(1 mark)**

b. We don't want to (represent) .... the
facts by exaggerating. **(1 mark)**

c. Please don't (agree) .... with me
because you know I'm right! **(1 mark)**

d. The whole thing has been a total (understanding)
.... **(1 mark)**

e. I think you have (interpreted) .... what
I was trying to say. **(1 mark)**

4 If you add the prefix **mal** to the word 'odorous', you make the word 'malodorous' meaning 'bad smelling'.

Add **mal** to the word 'practice' and you get 'malpractice' meaning 'bad practice'.

Now work out what **malfunction** means. **(1 mark)**

....

5 Tick the **two** sentences that use **prefixes** correctly. **(2 marks)**

a. I think the football team were somewhat disguided by their coach. ☐

b. The teacher said my artwork was incomplete. ☐

c. Although the puppies are from the same litter, they are quite unsimilar. ☐

d. It is quite improbable that the stadium will be finished by next year. ☐

Prefixes from Latin and Greek

1 What do these **prefixes** mean?

a. bi e.g. **bi**-lingual; **bi**cycle .... **(1 mark)**

b. super e.g. **super**market; **super**human .... **(1 mark)**

c. tele e.g. **tele**scope; **tele**vision .... **(1 mark)**

d. semi e.g. **semi**-circle; **semi**-detached .... **(1 mark)**

2 How many words can you think of that begin with the prefixes **auto**, **aqua** and **pre**?

(12 marks)

auto		aqua	pre
....	....	....	....
....	....	....	....
....	....	....	....

Top tip! Anything with **anti** as its prefix is going to have an opposite meaning to the original word. 'Anti-clockwise' means the opposite to 'clockwise'.

Total 31

1 What is a **suffix**? (1 mark)

....

....

2 Add the suffixes **able** and **ably** to these words, to make adjectives and adverbs.

	Adjective	Adverb
depend	....	....
comfort	....	....
rely	....	....
notice	....	....

(4 marks)

3 Add the suffixes **ible** and **ibly** to these words to make adjectives and adverbs. (5 marks)

	Adjective	Adverb
horror	....	....
terror	....	....
sense	....	....
reverse	....	....
audio	....	....

4 Add the suffix **cious** to turn these nouns into adjectives.

  a. vice .... **(1 mark)**

  b. malice .... **(1 mark)**

  c. space .... **(1 mark)**

  d. grace .... **(1 mark)**

5 Add the suffix **tious** to turn these nouns into adjectives.

  a. ambition .... **(1 mark)**

  b. infection .... **(1 mark)**

  c. nutrition .... **(1 mark)**

  d. fiction .... **(1 mark)**

Total $\frac{}{18}$

1 Rewrite the following sentences using either the suffix **tial** or **cial** to turn the nouns in bold into adjectives.

a. We went on our Year 6 (**residence**) trip to the Lake District.

(1 mark)

....

b. After so many (**finance**) worries, the Head Teacher was relieved he could afford the PE equipment. **(1 mark)**

....

c. Many people believed the teacher had been very (**influence**) in inspiring the children. **(1 mark)**

....

d. The cheeky boy pulled different (**face**) expressions as the teacher talked. **(1 mark)**

....

2 Choose either the suffix **ence** or **ance** to change these words into nouns that you cannot see or touch.

a. innocent .... **(1 mark)**

b. defend .... **(1 mark)**

c. dominate .... **(1 mark)**

d. tolerate .... **(1 mark)**

e. hesitate .... **(1 mark)**

f. obedient .... **(1 mark)**

3 Change these verbs into nouns by adding either the suffix **ence** or **ance**.

a. Walking in the Peak District was a real (**endure**) test.

.... **(1 mark)**

If a noun is formed from a verb ending in **y**, **ure** or **ear**, the ending of the noun will be **ance**. If a noun is formed from a verb ending in **ere** or **er**, the ending of the noun will be **ence**.

Top tip!

b. The Head Teacher thanked us for our (**comply**) with the school uniform rule.

.... **(1 mark)**

c. My (**rely**) on my brother to help me with my homework has got to stop!

.... **(1 mark)**

d. The instructions said that after the (**apply**) of glue, the two sides would stick together.

.... **(1 mark)**

e. After much (**reassure**) from my friends, I felt able to confront the bully.

.... **(1 mark)**

f. The (**disappear**) of our dog in the middle of the night was a complete mystery.

.... **(1 mark)**

4 Turn the following words into nouns by adding either the suffix **ence** or **ance**.

a. interfere .... **(1 mark)**

b. persevere .... **(1 mark)**

c. adhere .... **(1 mark)**

Suffixes from Greek

1 Write a word that includes each of the suffixes **phone**, **meter**, **logy** and **phobia**, then write its meaning. **(8 marks)**

Suffix	Word	Meaning
phone	....	....
meter	....	....
logy	....	....
phobia	....	....

Total — 27

The rule 'i before e except after c but only when it rhymes with bee'

1 Write six words that follow the rule 'i before e except after c but only when it rhymes with bee'. **(6 marks)**

....

....

....

2 Underline the correct spelling of the words in brackets in these sentences.

a. After searching high and low, I eventually found my (receipt / reciept). **(1 mark)**

b. I didn't want to (decieve / deceive) my mum so I told her about the torn book. **(1 mark)**

c. The teachers (percieved / perceived) that the child had been bullied. **(1 mark)**

d. My dad pulled a muscle in his back while painting the (cieling / ceiling). **(1 mark)**

e. The idea was (conceived / concieved) by the student council members. **(1 mark)**

f. The Queen was graciously (received / recieved) by the Fijian islanders. **(1 mark)**

Top tip!

Although it's a good idea to remember the rule 'i before e except after c but only when it rhymes with bee', you must learn the exceptions too! Here are some examples:

beige   feign   foreign   forfeit   height
neighbour   vein   weight

3 The following anagrams are exceptions to the rule 'i before e except after c, but only when it rhymes with bee'. Write the correctly spelled word next to the anagram.

a. eghit .... **(1 mark)**

b. hitweg .... **(1 mark)**

c. beegi .... **(1 mark)**

d. driew .... **(1 mark)**

e. tropien .... **(1 mark)**

f. finecafe .... **(1 mark)**

Words ending in fer

1 Add the suffixes **al**, **ence** and **ed** to the words on the left, then tick the correct box to indicate whether the **fer** sound is stressed or unstressed. **(10 marks)**

Word	Add suffixes	Is the **fer** stressed? ✓/✗
refer	**al**:..	
	ence:..	
	ed:..	
transfer	**al**:..	
	ence:..	
	ed:..	
prefer	**ence**:..	
	ed:..	
infer	**ence**:..	
	ed:..	

Total $\frac{}{28}$

Letter string ough

❶ Complete the table with as many words as you can find containing the letter string **ough**, matching the words to the sounds indicated in the column headings. One word for each has been done for you.

(1 mark per word)

oh sound	**aw** sound	**uff** sound	**ow** sound	**o** sound
though	*bought*	*enough*	*bough*	*cough*
....	....	....	....	....
....	....	....	....	....

❷ The words underlined in these sentences have been spelled as they sound. Rewrite them, correcting the words by using the **ough** letter string.

a. My brother <u>brawt</u> me some <u>coff</u> medicine because he <u>thawt</u> it would make me better. **(1 mark)**

....

b. The <u>ruff</u> seas were bad <u>enuf</u> but once on land, a <u>bow</u> from a <u>tuff</u> old oak tree snapped and landed on my head. **(1 mark)**

....

Silent letters

❶ Explain what is meant by a **silent letter**. **(1 mark)**

....

❷ Underline the **silent letters** in the following words. **(12 marks)**

a. assign

b. debt

c. crumb

d. nestle

e. condemn

f. honest

g. foreign

h. sword

i. knowledge

j. hymn

k. scissors

l. receipt

3 The words in bold in the following sentences have had their silent letters removed. Rewrite the words using the correct spelling.

a. Last **Wenesday** I went to buy some new **hankerchiefs** in town. **(1 mark)**

....

b. Despite the **josling** crowds, I finally bought a card with a **silouette** of a flower in the corner. **(1 mark)**

....

c. I put my **receit** safely in my bag and had a drink before **succuming** to the rush hour traffic. **(1 mark)**

....

d. The songs we sang were quite **solem** and **ecoed** around the hall. **(1 mark)**

....

The prefix psych

1 In the following words, the prefix **psych** has become separated from the rest of word, which is an anagram.
Unravel the root words and join them to the prefix **psych** to make the correct word.

a. psych gooly   .... **(1 mark)**

b. psych tristia   .... **(1 mark)**

c. psych ci   .... **(1 mark)**

d. psych delice   .... **(1 mark)**

The letters ph

1 How many words can you list that either begin with **ph** or have **ph** in them?

(up to 12 marks)

....	....	....
....	....	....
....	....	....
....	....	....

Total $\frac{}{44}$

Words ending in o

❶ Write the **plurals** of the following words.   **(9 marks)**

Singular	Plural
piano	....
hero	....
mango	....
studio	....
banjo	....
echo	....
kilo	....
potato	....
torpedo	....

Words ending in f, ff and fe

❶ Change the words in brackets from **singular to plural**.

    a. My dad put up some new (shelf) in my bedroom.

    ....   **(1 mark)**

    b. We had to buy some new (knife) as the old ones were blunt.

    ....   **(1 mark)**

    c. Our (life) have changed dramatically since we got our puppy.

    ....   **(1 mark)**

    d. All through the night we heard the howls of (wolf).

    ....   **(1 mark)**

    e. We heard there had been (thief) in our school last night.

    ....   **(1 mark)**

2 Rewrite the sentences below, changing the underlined singular nouns ending in **f** or **ff** to the **plural**.

a. The tribal <u>chief</u> agreed to respect each other's different <u>belief</u>. **(1 mark)**

....

b. From the top of the <u>roof</u> came billowing <u>puff</u> of white smoke. **(1 mark)**

....

c. The pirate's <u>bluff</u> had gone on long enough so the captain dropped anchor in front of the towering white <u>cliff</u> and confronted him. **(1 mark)**

....

....

d. The garden party <u>chef</u> put on <u>waterproof</u> when it started to rain. **(1 mark)**

....

e. The little <u>waif</u> were poorly dressed and underfed after being looked after by two beastly <u>oaf</u>. **(1 mark)**

....

Words with two possible plurals

1 Write both plural forms of these singular nouns. **(4 marks)**

Singular	Plural 1	Plural 2
scarf		
wharf		
dwarf		
hoof		

Total $\frac{}{23}$

Homophones

1 Write a definition for the word **homophone**. **(1 mark)**

....

2 Each of the following sentences contains words in bold that are homophones. Tick the **one** which has used the right ones. **(1 mark)**

a. We weren't **aloud** to **waist** food as Mum was always very conscious of people who were starving. ☐

b. There was a **pear** of shoes on the **stares** that I had never seen before. ☐

c. I couldn't **bare** him when we were growing up but now we are **to** old to squabble. ☐

d. I looked **through** the window and saw a huge **bear** ambling about in the garden. ☐

3 Match these words up with a homophone. For some, you may find more than one. **(14 marks)**

Word	Homophone(s)	Word	Homophone(s)
pause	....	whether	....
piece	....	find	....
pour	....	great	....
knew	....	flower	....
buy	....	night	....
morning	....	sent	....
profit	....	root	....

Near homophones

1 Explain what **near homophones** are. **(1 mark)**

....

2 Circle the **correct** word in the following sentences.

a. The hot, sunny weather had a therapeutic **effect / affect** on the whole family. **(1 mark)**

b. The teacher gave the parents some great **advise / advice** about the tests. **(1 mark)**

c. The fireman couldn't gain **access / excess** to the burning building. **(1 mark)**

d. Last night the pool was full of screaming **adolescents / adolescence**. **(1 mark)**

e. I bought the latest **edition / addition** of my favourite magazine. **(1 mark)**

f. We all found it difficult to **accept / except** that our cat had gone. **(1 mark)**

Homonyms

1 What are **homonyms**? **(1 mark)**

....

2 Write two sentences using each **homonym** to show their different meanings.

a. watch **(2 marks)**

  i. ....

  ii. ....

b. bark **(2 marks)**

  i. ....

  ii. ....

c. train **(2 marks)**

  i. ....

  ii. ....

d. fair **(2 marks)**

  i. ....

  ii. ....

Top tip!

To help you remember **practice / practise:** **practice** with a **c** is a **noun**; **c** comes before **n** in the alphabet; **practise** with an **s** is a **verb**; **s** comes before **v** in the alphabet.

This also works with **advice / advise** too!

Total $\frac{}{32}$

① Underline the most suitable **conjunction** from the list to complete this sentence. **(1 mark)**

*Hassan played basketball...
having a sore wrist.*

because   despite   however   since

② Tick **one** word to make the sentence below grammatically correct. **(1 mark)**

My little brother .... when he was running in the park.

falled ☐

falls ☐

felled ☐

fell ☐

③ Which word is an **antonym** for **sensible**? Tick **one**. **(1 mark)**

lively ☐

irresponsible ☐

calm ☐

practical ☐

④ Tick the **one** sentence that uses the correct **plural**. **(1 mark)**

Did you see those womens running on the track? ☐

There were six gooses waddling down the road. ☐

The polite man stood up to let the old ladys sit down. ☐

The thieves were arrested as they tried to leave town. ☐

5 Underline one **fronted adverbial** and one **adverb** in this sentence. **(1 mark)**

Cautiously, the boys crept into the cave, treading carefully as they went.

6 Complete this sentence using suitable **pronouns**. **(1 mark)**

When .... arrived at our mother's bedside,

.... could see that .... had greatly improved.

7 Label the words below as either **nouns** or **adjectives**. **(1 mark)**

Phil studied the detailed map then put it back neatly in his waterproof rucksack.

8 Which sentence is an **exclamation**? Tick **one**. **(1 mark)**

Follow me quickly! ☐

How many people do you want to invite? ☐

What a fuss about nothing! ☐

I'm walking home now. ☐

9 Replace the underlined word with a **synonym**. Write the new word in the box. **(1 mark)**

After four laps of the field and a game of hockey, we were all <u>tired</u>.

10 Underline the **conjunction** that makes most sense in each pair of brackets.

(1 mark)

Our football team finally won (after / since) many defeats, (therefore / however) we know we have a long way to go before we can claim the league cup.

11 Which **two** sentences have **subject–verb** agreement? Tick **two**.　　**(1 mark)**

My two younger sisters eats toast and jam for supper.　☐

All the others apart from Joe takes the bus to school.　☐

Ushma's dog teases my cats.　☐

With two more exams left, we was still working very hard.　☐

They were swimming in the sea early this morning.　☐

12 Complete the sentence below with a suitable **contraction**.

I always loved the end of term when .... finished our exams and the days were long.　**(1 mark)**

13 Circle the **conjunction** in the sentence below.　　**(1 mark)**

My younger brother loves peas yet hates carrots.

14 Insert a pair of **brackets** around the part of the sentence that adds extra information.

a. My cousin the one from America is always talking about celebrities.　**(1 mark)**

b. When I get home in the evening no matter how late I like to relax with a book.　**(1 mark)**

c. The summer holiday months July and August are a great time to visit the Lake District.　**(1 mark)**

d. The Head Teacher laughed happily not a common sight I can tell you during the Year 6 production. **(1 mark)**

15 Insert a pair of **commas** to show where a **parenthesis** has been inserted in the sentence. **(1 mark)**

The family we met on holiday all of whom were very pleasant contacted us last week.

16 Underline the **verbs** in the **present tense**.

a. We love to visit the seaside but last year it was a bit of a washout.

(1 mark)

b. My dog liked our long walks when he was young but lately he becomes very tired. **(1 mark)**

c. All through the school year, we worked hard but now is the time to relax.

(1 mark)

17 Underline the **subordinate clause** in the sentence below. **(1 mark)**

My brother went to school today, despite having his arm in plaster.

18 Underline the **phrase** in this sentence that tells you it is a **question**. **(1 mark)**

"So you think you're going to win the match tomorrow, do you?"

19 Add **inverted commas** to this dialogue. **(1 mark)**

Hurry up or you'll be late for school! shouted my mum.
It's almost 9 o'clock.
Why don't we take the short cut through the field?
I asked. We'd be there in no time.

20 Add **apostrophes** to show contraction and possession in the following sentences.

   a. Abbys cat has gone missing but hes wearing his blue collar so hell be easily spotted. **(1 mark)**

   b. Mums been waiting ages for Katies bus but its clearly late. **(1 mark)**

   c. Were so thrilled that Jakes passed his exams that we think itd be good to celebrate. **(1 mark)**

21 Match each group of words to the correct grammar term. **(1 mark)**

she flew up the stairs	relative clause
who used to be my teacher	main clause
some buried treasure	expanded noun phrase

22 Which sentence is grammatically correct? Tick **one**. **(1 mark)**

   Erin's pencil case is more fuller than Sian's. ☐

   Stella's reading is more advanced than Chloe's. ☐

   Jordan's dog is more viciouser than Ahmed's. ☐

   Our homework is more harder than yours. ☐

23 Add a **colon** to the sentence below. **(1 mark)**

   When I pack for a weekend away in the countryside, I take lots of warm clothes sweaters, boots, gloves and a coat.

24 Complete the sentence below with the correct form of the verb **to eat**. **(1 mark)**

   After having .... our breakfast, we jumped into the car and headed off.

25 Choose a word from the list below to complete this sentence so that it is in the **subjunctive mood**.

I wish I .... better at cooking so I could help you in the kitchen when we have visitors.

Tick **one**.

did ☐   **(1 mark)**

might be ☐   **(1 mark)**

was ☐   **(1 mark)**

were ☐   **(1 mark)**

26 Which event is the **most likely** to happen? Tick **one**.   **(1 mark)**

I will finish my homework project this evening. ☐

Orla might be going to the library with her mum. ☐

The forecaster said that it could snow later on. ☐

I can drop your book off at around 9 o'clock. ☐

27 Use the **conjunctions** in the box to complete the sentence below. Use each conjunction **once**.   **(1 mark)**

but	or	even though	and

You need to water the flowers .... the plants,

.... it rained in the night. Here is a watering can

.... you might prefer to use a jug .... a hose.

28 Complete this sentence by adding a **question tag**. **(1 mark)**

You need to get a move on or you'll be late ....

29 Explain the meaning of each sentence, where one has a comma and the other does not. **(1 mark)**

Shall we start to eat, Mum?

Shall we start to eat Mum?

....

....

....

30 Add a **comma** to the sentence below. **(1 mark)**

After an extremely long flight I was relieved to get into my comfortable bed for a sleep.

31 Joe likes making cheese sandwiches. The ingredients he uses are bread, cheese and butter. His brother asks him to write down the recipe so he can make one too.

Finish the recipe that Joe has started, using **bullet points** to write the ingredients in a list. Remember to use the correct **punctuation**. **(1 mark)**

To make your cheese sandwich, you will need the following ....

....

....

....

32 Insert a **contraction** into the sentence below. **(1 mark)**

There isn't time for us to eat because .... already 9 o'clock.

33 Put one letter in each box to show what type of word each one is. **(1 mark)**

noun A	adverb B	verb C	proper noun D	adjective E

Mrs Courtney's antique vase suddenly tipped over.

34 There is a **grammatical error** in this sentence. Write the corrected sentence on the line below.

(1 mark)

After a long day in the park, the exhausted children was glad to get home.

....

35 Put a tick in each row to show how the **apostrophe** has been used in each sentence. An example has been done for you. **(4 marks)**

Sentence	Apostrophe used in a contraction	Apostrophe used to show possession
There's not a lot of room in here.	✓	
I daren't tell the teacher I forgot my homework.		
Rebecca's pony likes apples.		
The children's books are in the library.		
We've been told to stand outside the office.		

36 Add a **prefix** from the box below to give this word a negative meaning.

(1 mark)

.....................................legal

in	il	mis	dis	un

37 Underline the correct form of the verb in each set of brackets. **(3 marks)**

A volcano is a mountain that (opens / is opening) downward to molten rock lying below the surface of the Earth. With the build-up of pressure, eruptions (occurred / occur). Gases and rock (shoots / shoot) up through the opening, filling the air with fragments of lava.

38 Tick the word that is closest in meaning to **mishap**. **(1 mark)**

unhappiness ☐

accident ☐

distortion ☐

trick ☐

39 Underline the two words in the passage below that show a **command**.

(1 mark)

Turn to the next page and read the first two paragraphs. What do you think made Theo react that way?

40 Insert an **apostrophe** in the sentence below to show **possession**.

Mrs Rothwells computer screen needed to be fixed. **(1 mark)**

Active voice – The subject of the sentence is doing or being; the object is having it done to them/it

Adjective – A word that describes a noun

Adverb – A word that tells us more about a verb or an adjective

Adverbial – An adverb that tells us where, when or how often something happens

Ambiguity – Having more than one meaning

Antonym – A word that means the opposite to another word

Apostrophe – A punctuation mark used to show omission (contraction) or possession

Brackets – Can show parenthesis

Bullet points – Used to draw attention to items in a list

Capital letters – Letters in upper case, used at the start of sentences and proper nouns

Clause – Contains a verb and can act as a sentence. It can be a main clause or subordinate clause

Colon – Introduces a clause that gives detail or introduces a list, a quotation or speech in a play script

Comma – Punctuation mark used to separate items in a list, in direct speech, show a brief pause, separate a main clause from a subordinate clause and to indicate parenthesis

Command – Gives an instruction

Common nouns – Nouns for people, animals and objects

Conjunction – Links two words, phrases or clauses

Context – The situation in which something happens

Contraction – A word that has been made shorter

Dash – A single dash shows a break or pause in a sentence

Dashes – Can show parenthesis

Definite article – The word 'the'

Determiner – A word that introduces a noun such as 'the', 'a', 'some' and 'those'

Dialogue – Conversation between two or more people

Direct speech – A sentence in inverted commas showing the exact words spoken by someone

Ellipsis – To show missing text

Emphasis – Stress

Exclamation – A forceful sentence that can express surprise, shock, strong emotion, pain or a warning

Exclamation mark – Punctuation at the end of an exclamation or command

Expanded noun phrase – A phrase with a noun as its main word with other words that tell us more about that noun

Formal speech – Speaking and writing using correct grammar and vocabulary

Fronted adverbial – An adverbial that comes at the front, or start, of a sentence

Full stops – Punctuation at the end of a sentence

Future – A verb tense saying what is going to happen

Homonyms – Words that sound the same and are spelled the same but have different meanings

Homophones – Words that sound the same but have a different spelling and different meanings

Hyphen – A punctuation mark that links words to make some compound words, to join prefixes to some words or to show a word break at the end of a line

Hyphenated compound words – Two words combined with a hyphen to make one new word

Informal speech and writing – Relaxed, chatty way of speaking and writing used with family and friends

Inverted commas – The punctuation at the start and end of speech

Main clause – A clause that can make sense as a sentence

Modal verbs – Verbs that show possibility or likelihood

Noun phrase – A phrase where a noun is the main word

Nouns – Naming words for people, places, animals and things

Object – A noun, pronoun or noun phrase

Omission – Leaving a letter or letters out

Parentheses – The plural form of parenthesis. It can also mean the punctuation marks themselves

Parenthesis – Keeping a word, phrase or clause separate from the rest of a sentence

Passive voice – When the subject isn't carrying out the action but is being acted upon by someone or something

Past – A verb tense saying what has happened

Personal pronoun – A word that replaces a noun

Phrase – A group of words that work together as if they are one word

Possession – Ownership

Possessive pronoun – A word to show ownership

Prefix – A string of letters added to the start of a word to change its meaning

Preposition – Shows the relationship between the noun or pronoun and other words in the clause or sentence

Present – A verb tense saying what is happening now

Proper nouns – Nouns that name particular things. They begin with a capital letter

Punctuation marks – 'Signposts' to help us understand text

Question – A sentence that asks something

Question mark – Punctuation mark at the end of a question

Relative clause – A subordinate clause introduced by a relative pronoun

Relative pronoun – The words 'who', 'which', 'that' and 'whose' which introduce a relative clause

Root word – A word in its own right, without a prefix or a suffix

Semi-colon – Links two closely related sentences or separates items in a list where some items might be longer than one or two words

Silent letter – A letter that was once pronounced but now isn't

Standard English – Using the rules of English correctly

Statement – A sentence that gives information

Stress – When you either increase the vowel length or loudness of the syllable or both

Subject – The person or thing that is doing or being something in the sentence

Subjunctive – A verb form that shows a wish or an imaginary state

Subordinate clause – A clause which depends on the main clause to make sense

Suffix – A string of letters added to the root word to change or add to its meaning

Syllable – A single, unbroken sound

Synonym – A word that means the same or almost the same as another word

Thesaurus – A book of words and their synonyms

Verb – A word for an action or state of being